A Narrative of

Thomas Smallwood

(Coloured Man)

# A Narrative of Thomas Smallwood

(Coloured Man)

## by Thomas Smallwood

Edited, Annotated, and with an Introduction

by Richard Almonte

THE MERCURY PRESS

The publisher gratefully acknowledges the financial assistance of the Canada Council for the Arts and the Ontario Arts Council. The publisher further acknowledges the financial support of the Government of Canada through the Department of Canadian Heritage's Book Publishing Industry Development Program (BPIDP) for our publishing activities.

Editor for the press: Beverley Daurio
Composition and page design by TASK
Printed and bound in Canada
Printed on acid-free paper

1 2 3 4 5 04 03 02 01 00

Canadian Cataloguing in Publication Data

Smallwood, Thomas
A narrative of Thomas Smallwood
ISBN 1-55128-082-5
1. Smallwood, Thomas. 2. Slavery - United States - History - 19th century. 3. Underground railroad. 4. Slaves - United States - Biography. 5. Blacks - Ontario - Biography. I. Almonte, Richard. II. Title.
E450.S65 2000 973.7'115'092 C00-932199-3

The Mercury Press
www.themercurypress.com

*For my grandparents*

Panfilo Almonte
Giuseppina Almonte
Stanislaw Bielinski
Zofia Bielinski

# CONTENTS

# INTRODUCTION

## ONE

The little that is known about Thomas Smallwood, or that has been written about him, comes from a total of five published sources. The first and most important source is his *Narrative*, published in Toronto in 1851. The second, though chronologically the first mention, of Smallwood in print, is in the document located in this book's Appendix, the *Report of the Convention of the Coloured Population, Held at Drummondville*, at which Smallwood participated vocally. Smallwood's and his family's irregular appearance in the annual Toronto City Directory after 1846 is our next substantial clue to his life. There is a mention of Smallwood in the biography of Mary Shadd, another Black Canadian writer of the 1850s; and finally, a complimentary mention of Smallwood and his *Narrative* in Charles T. Davis' and Henry Louis Gates, Jr.'s *The Slave's Narrative*. The first section of this Introduction examines these five clues in order to arrive at a partial picture of the only ex-slave to publish his narrative in Canada. The last two sections address the generic status, thematic concerns, and figurative language of the *Narrative*, and its national literary context.

The 1851 edition of Smallwood's *Narrative* is 73 densely-packed pages long. Of this total amount, only one or two pages can rightly be said to deal with biographical matters. Thus, the subtitle of the original 1851 edition: "Giving an account of his birth— the period he was held in slavery— his release— and removal to Canada, etc., Together with an account of the Underground Railroad," is arguably misleading. While we have no way of knowing whether it was Smallwood, or James Stephens, his publisher, who decided on the misleading cover-copy, it is fairly certain that both men would have been lead by the same motive in their choice. The decision to highlight the biographical portion of the *Narrative* played to the reading public's interest in slave narratives that described, often graphically, the brutality of slavery. Readers of the *Narrative* will notice, however, that Smallwood makes a conscious choice to underplay his experience as a slave, and his biography in general. Smallwood's experience as a slave is dealt with in one paragraph, and then never mentioned again. His choice of language and rhetoric in this opening paragraph is subtle and skillful. "I was recorded to be set free," Smallwood writes, "at the age of thirty," thus defamilarizing the experience of slavery precisely by not naming it. Instead, Smallwood concentrates on his eventual freedom. Smallwood mentions his wife only a handful of times, does not mention his children, does not mention the kind of work he does or where he lives; nor does he describe the person or the event that has caused him to write the *Narrative.*

Luckily, the *Narrative* does contain some of the dates most vital in formulating a basic chronology of Smallwood's life. Born in 1801, marries in 1830, purchases freedom in 1831, active in Underground Railroad between 1831 and 1843, emigrates to Canada in 1843.

To get a less impersonal glimpse of Smallwood's activity in the period between his emigration to Canada and his publishing of the *Narrative,* we can turn to the *Report of the Convention of the Coloured Population, Held at Drummondville,* a slim 16-page pamphlet published in Toronto in 1847. This pamphlet is evidence of the first meeting held in Canada west of Nova Scotia solely devoted to the concerns of the Black community. Smallwood sat on the nominating, business and finance committees of the Drummondville (the town that is present-day Niagara Falls) convention, which was attended by other well-known leaders of the Black Canadian community, like Josiah Henson. In fact, the convention is noteworthy because it constituted a sort of showdown between a faction led by Smallwood on one side and Henson on the other side over the issue of Henson's role in the Dawn settlement, near Chatham. Smallwood implied in motions made on the floor of the convention that Henson was pocketing an unduly large percentage of the monies he had collected as agent for the Dawn settlement. Smallwood is very prominent in the *Report*: he is listed first among participants, and intriguingly, his name is prefaced by the title "Rev.," signalling that Smallwood has left another important piece of information out of his *Narrative*, namely that he worked as a minister.

The most accessible source that provides a sense of Smallwood's life in Canada is the Toronto City Directory, a reference work published annually beginning in 1834. Like early but more-detailed Yellow Pages, the city directories contain basic information on every adult inhabitant of the city. The directories are important for a number of reasons. From them, we are able to construct Smallwood's movements within the city over time: both his home address and business address changed a number of times during his life. In addition, the city directory tells us what type of work Smallwood did. The city directory allows us also to sketch in the shadowy figures of Smallwood's family: his children, and their occupations. Smallwood appears in the directory for the first time in 1846. His listing is as follows: "Smallwood Thomas, (coloured) labourer, 82 York-st." Smallwood's last appearance in the directory is in 1883, this time listed as "Smallwood Thos, saw setter, h 18 Elizabeth." Smallwood, who appears to have lived to be 82 years old, moved over five times in those 37 years. He lived for the majority of those years in an area defined loosely by Queen Street to the south, Dundas Street to the north, Bay Street to the east, and University Avenue to the west, with a business address adjacent to his home address. Smallwood's children, among them Joseph, a plasterer, Thomas, a sawdresser and later bricklayer, Virginia, a hairdresser, and William, a law student, bookkeeper, and later owner of a bicycle company, fill in the incomplete picture Smallwood paints of his family life in the *Narrative*.

The final two published sources that provide information on Smallwood are secondary sources. In their biography, *Shadd: The Life and Times of Mary Shadd Cary*, Jim Bearden and Linda Jean Butler discover that the newspaper edited and published by Shadd Cary, the *Provincial Freeman*, was sued by its shareholders, among whom was Thomas Smallwood. Smallwood, "a Toronto businessman... led a court action against the *Freeman* to force payment due shareholders: payment the *Freeman* could ill afford."(192) This fact, when added to Smallwood's insistence that the *Narrative* was written to clear his name, as well as Smallwood's acrimonious exchange with Josiah Henson at the Drummondville convention, might lead us to see Smallwood (to put it charitably) as a person who was involved in a number of disputes. Alternately, we might choose to say that Smallwood found himself, by virtue of being a leading member of the Black community, inevitably drawn into disputes. The point is that Smallwood's life demonstrates that the nineteenth-century Black Canadian community should not be seen— as it often is in popular Canadian history— as a uniform group of ex-slaves happy simply to be in Canada.

Finally, in *The Slave's Narrative*, Charles T. Davis and Henry Louis Gates, Jr. discuss Smallwood as a writer. Published in 1985, *The Slave's Narrative* solidified the acceptance of the slave narrative as a major genre in American literature. Davis' and Gates, Jr.'s wide-ranging collection has been very influential in almost all subsequent work on the American slave narrative. Two aspects of Davis' and Gates, Jr.'s treatment of Smallwood and the *Narrative* are instructive. While placing Smallwood alongside much better known writers of slave narratives, such as Frederick Douglass, the authors claim surprise that his book has not become better known: "even the most diligent historians"(xxix) have forgotten it. This comment almost begs the question of why it is that Smallwood's *Narrative* has been forgotten. Davis and Gates, Jr. go on to position Smallwood's as a proto-typical slave narrative because of its examination of "the direct relationship between freedom and discourse"(xxv); Smallwood is praised for demonstrating a Black desire for progress, which is directly linked to the ability to read and write. "No one," Davis and Gates, Jr. argue, "puts this more aptly than Thomas Smallwood."(xxix) In the next section, which offers a reading of the *Narrative*, this direct link will be problematized.

## TWO

Smallwood's *Narrative* does not fit as comfortably into the genre of American slave narrative as Davis and Gates, Jr. would have their readers believe. Two factors stand out especially: the book's national status, and its thematic and rhetorical concerns. The former factor will be discussed in the third section of this Introduction. This section describes the thematic concerns and rhetoric of the *Narrative* in order to argue that Smallwood appropriates the slave narrative genre— which he realizes is powerful and guaranteed of an audience— for his own ends. Smallwood's aims run directly against, in some instances, the generally agreed upon aims of the American slave narrative. Smallwood's overwhelming interest in demonstrating the treachery that exists between various members of the Black community is the main theme of the *Narrative*. To see how Smallwood writes against the tradition, we must first examine the way in which slave narratives have been inscribed generically.

James Olney's essay "'I Was Born': Slave Narratives, Their Status as Autobiography and as Literature," included in the Davis and Gates, Jr. collection, has had a profound impact on the way in which slave narratives have been read and taught. Olney's essay provides a taxonomy of the genre, including a generical "master outline"(152) of plot events and devices that Olney argues can be applied to any slave narrative. Not surprisingly, Olney's taxonomy bears out a rather reductive conclusion. According to Olney, slave narratives are "always" about "the realities of the institution of slavery" and "almost never the intellectual, emotional, moral growth of the narrator."(154) Olney's position has received gentle criticism from Jennifer Fleischner, whose recent book, *Mastering Slavery: Memory, Family, and Identity in Women's Slave Narratives*, seeks to re-evaluate women's slave narratives precisely from a space of "differentiated memories... idiosyncrasies of theme... autobiographical commitment."(15) Fleischner finds Olney's point of view "insightful"(14) but claims that "there are limitations to the premise that these narratives are shaped by and reflect nothing but cultural and ideological currents."(15) Smallwood's *Narrative* provides one such limitation.

Among Smallwood's rhetorical concerns mentioned at the beginning of this section, two stand out. First, the tension in the *Narrative* between the need to deliver originality and authenticity, and the need to partake in a literary tradition, is unique. Smallwood's claim that the *Narrative* is "wholly original,"(30) as well as his lengthy digression in the Preface about the plagiarism of David Walker's *Appeal*, needs to be read in tandem with his self-conscious insertion of numerous quotations from famous British and American poets, including Milton and Shakespeare. These competing strategies show Smallwood to be a writer who is hyper-sensitive around his own authority, but at the same time who realizes that to some degree his authority rests on his ability to demonstrate his knowledge of other writers. Smallwood's foregrounding of plagiarism (by quoting Walker's *Appeal*) and authority (through numerous quotations from well-known poets) are integral to our understanding of the *Narrative*. Smallwood's use of these competing rhetorics does something new. It proclaims not only that Smallwood is authentic in detailing his life and his experiences, but also that he is authentic as an author, familiar with the great poets.

Olney argues that the theme, content, and form of slave narratives never change. When he deals with style and rhetoric it is to claim that some slave narratives that were ghost-written by white writers borrow heavily from "the sentimental rhetoric of white fiction."(164) This is part of Olney's larger thesis that the slave narrative exists in a "triangular relationship of narrator, audience, and sponsors."(154) In such a relationship, the slave narrative author is constrained by his white abolitionist audience's expectations, and therefore replicates the same narrative each time. The argument is tempting, but in denying the agency of the author, as well as the possibility that slave narrative readership is not solely white, it fails to encompass the numerous examples, Smallwood's being possibly the most important, of slave narratives that consciously work against the genre. Smallwood's regular deployment of sarcasm in the *Narrative* is instructive. By italicizing the phrase "grateful Republic"(81) near the end of the *Narrative*, or by describing the United States Congress as "magnanimous,"(70) Smallwood achieves a level of critique not often encountered in slave narrative.

Whereas Olney sees the theme of slave narratives as "the reality of slavery and the necessity of abolishing it,"(156) Smallwood's *Narrative* tells a different story. Smallwood's theme is the sad fact of what he calls "the treachery of some of our brethren" and the relationship of this treachery to "filthy lucre."(48) For Smallwood, treachery and greed are twin evils that have impeded the cause of anti-slavery. His *Narrative* is a denunciation of these evils, written in the form of an adventure story, with Smallwood cast in the role of the hero. Charles H. Nichols has demonstrated the usefulness of viewing the slave narrative protagonist as a picaresque hero, but where Nichols sees the "picaro-slave" demonstrating "contempt for the... master class,"(283) Smallwood demonstrates instead contempt for some members of his own Black community.

For Smallwood, greed is rampant in the Canadian Black community. He makes sure to rhetorically distance himself from the appearance of greed right at the beginning of the *Narrative*. "Let no one suppose," he writes, "that I have written this for the sake of pecuniary gain."(34) A few pages later we begin to understand Smallwood's desire that his *Narrative* "clear up [his] character."(27) He mentions that he has been charged, by some of the people he has helped free from slavery, "with taking an undue amount of money from them."(41) Smallwood protests his innocence, carefully making the protest after he has recounted a particularly dangerous (to himself) instance of effecting a slave escape:

> These then were the times if I was a traitor to my brethren, with which my enemies have attempted to brand me, when I could have made my jack. But it is passing strange, and not to be credited by any reasonable, just, and unprejudiced person, that I should for a paltry sum of a few dollars or pounds become an enemy to my brethren for whom I have almost worn myself out.(45)

Almost every mention of treachery in the *Narrative* is followed by some reference to money. Smallwood's numerous injunctions against greed, countered by his positioning of himself as a self-made man impervious to the temptations of greed, argue against Olney's easy dismissal of slave narratives as containing "conventions untransformed and unredeemed."(158)

## THREE

There are other thematic and rhetorical concerns that contribute to a full reading of the *Narrative*, including Smallwood's depiction of women, and the language he uses to describe women, his use of the concept of "race," as well as his invocation of God on numerous occasions. What is especially of interest here, though, is the textual and extra-textual relationship between the *Narrative* and its material background. Simply put, the slave narrative is a literary genre of the United States. Smallwood's *Narrative*, as the sole example of a slave narrative written and published in Canada, contests this American generic hegemony. Unlike a number of other Black writers with "Canadian periods" who eventually moved back to the United States or elsewhere (Mary Shadd Cary, Martin Delany, Samuel Ringgold Ward), Smallwood lived out the second half of his life in Canada. Where then do Smallwood as a writer, and the *Narrative* as a nineteenth-century text, find a home?

By the most basic criteria— the author's place of residence, and the text's place of publication— Smallwood's *Narrative* is a Canadian book. As mentioned above though, the *Narrative* is firmly rooted in an American literary genre, the slave narrative. To disentangle this literary knot is to participate in the incipient and closely-contested debate between scholars over the positioning of Black Canadian culture. At first glance, the *Narrative* appears to be a perfect example of what George Elliott Clarke has termed "cultural self-inscription."(56) In his essay, "Must All Blackness Be American?: Locating Canada in Borden's *Tightrope Time*, or Nationalizing Gilroy's *The Black Atlantic*," Clarke proposes that "African-Canadian literature"(56) is produced through a process whereby Canadian writers signify on African-American texts and writers.

Clarke's reading of Walter Borden's play *Tightrope Time* effectively demonstrates that Borden's play is an imaginative re-telling of American playwright Lorraine Hansberry's well-known play *A Raisin in the Sun*. Clarke's language in this essay is telling. Borden "sounds the work" of Hansberry, "imports Hansberry directly into his work,"(66) "absorbs Hansberry's... musings and terms,"(61) and "teases from Hansberry"(62) various terms. Clarke's belaboured reading of Borden's play leaves no room for doubt: African-Canadian texts evolve directly out of African-American texts. We might say, then, using Clarke's thesis, that any Canadianness evinced by Smallwood's *Narrative* happens precisely in those moments when Smallwood deforms and reforms (Clarke's terms) the slave narrative tradition as formulated by Olney and others. Smallwood's deliberate writing into the narrative, for instance, of his sense of anger at being wrongly vilified by his own community, rewrites, in a Canadian way, the standard slave narrative where any hardships that occur occur strictly as a result of slavery.

There is, however, another side to the debate over Black Canadian culture. In "Rhetorics of Blackness, Rhetorics of Belonging: The Politics of Representation in Black Canadian Expressive Culture," Rinaldo Walcott argues for a different paradigm of Black Canadianness: Canadian Blackness as diasporic. For Walcott, diasporic Blackness, a "looking beyond national boundaries... is crucial for revisiting the imposition of nation-state narratives which seek to render Blackness as less than."(12) In this case, we might interpret Walcott's "less than" as being aimed directly at Clarke's conception of African-Canadian literature as being always somehow bound-up in earlier African-American literature. Walcott rejects "nativism" which he identifies with Clarke's criticism, "which understands Caribbean Blackness as occupying too much space."(12) A reading of Smallwood using Walcott's diasporic method would concentrate not so much on the generic concerns articulated earlier (can there be a Canadian slave narrative?) but rather on how the politics the text evinces *place* Smallwood in relation to other articulations of Canadian Blackness. For evidence of such placement, we return to the *Narrative*.

Smallwood's depiction of Canada, where he had lived for eight years by the time he published the *Narrative*, is contradictory. The language he uses to describe Canada initially is religious. He goes on a "pilgrimage" that ends in Toronto, "Queen City of the West," where he finds, unfortunately, "a prejudice equal to anything I ever experienced in the South."(27) A paragraph later, he uses the phrase "our city" to describe Toronto, inscribing a sense of pride and belonging that is echoed by Toronto being listed as the place of residence of the author at the end of the Preface, as well as the place of publication on the cover page. In the *Narrative*, however, it is difficult to get a precise explanation of this pride. More often than not, the description of Canada sounds like a cliché. Canada is the land of "free soil… true freedom… and equal laws."(53) A paragraph later, Canada is where "the laws are equal, and know no difference between man and man on account of colour." After admitting in the Preface that there is as much prejudice in Canada as in the States, Smallwood still hopes that, "Thanks to the laws, it may go no further than verbal illustration!"(27)

Smallwood's ambivalence towards Canada, encapsulated perfectly in the word "coloured" which appears in brackets on his title-page, both present and not-present, mirrors my own ambivalence over where and whether to "place" his book. Numerous simplifications inevitably occur when attempting such placement; simplifications I was happy to make in my introduction to Mary Shadd's *A Plea For Emigration*, but which now seem perhaps hasty. Reducing the current debate over Black Canadian culture to a nativist versus diasporic oppositional framework (as I've done above) is risky. It has the virtue of replicating a similar sort of debate to that which existed among Black Canadians in the nineteenth Century (see for example the Appendix), and thus of not propagating the myth that Canadian Blackness is or ever has been monolithic. Conversely, simplification of the debate has the effect of hiding the real crux of the matter, which is the political investment behind the diasporic and nativist stances, and the way these investments are either supported or not supported by the already established entities of Canadian literature and African-American literature. This is a topic that should be reserved for its own separate treatment.

## *A Note on the Text*

The text of Smallwood's *Narrative* presented below has been edited with one main consideration in mind: readability. Without making unnecessary changes to the original edition, a number of Smallwood's very long paragraphs have been divided into smaller units. Similarly, a number of Smallwood's longer sentences (he had a propensity for the many-claused sentence) have been simplified. Other than that, the original 1851 edition is engagingly written and well-printed, and there are few other errors (spelling, for example) to correct. Unlike in a scholarly edition, where each of the editor's changes are listed in a separate apparatus to remove the possibility of bias, this edition hides its editor's choices, assuming the reader will indulge any bias that exists. Because Smallwood's *Narrative* was published only once, and because no manuscript copy exists, the need for textual comparison between editions— another important component of scholarly editions— does not exist either. Readers who would like to compare this edition to the original edition may consult the CIHM microfiche (56617) of the 1851 edition, available at most Canadian university libraries.

A

# NARRATIVE

OF

# THOMAS SMALLWOOD,

(Coloured Man:)

GIVING AN ACCOUNT

OF HIS

BIRTH—THE PERIOD HE WAS HELD IN SLAVERY—HIS RELEASE—AND REMOVAL TO CANADA, ETC.

TOGETHER WITH

AN ACCOUNT OF THE UNDERGROUND RAILROAD.

WRITTEN BY HIMSELF.

Toronto:

PRINTED FOR THE AUTHOR BY JAMES STEPHENS, 5, CITY BUILDINGS, KING STREET EAST.

1851.

# Preface

We live in stirring times! Perhaps in no period of the world's history, in the annals of no ancient clime, in no grand epoch of the past, have any strange events taken place to which the present century may not produce a loftier parallel. We may call back to remembrance those days that have gone to the winds, and glance our eyes over even to those far ages bordering on the flood. Traversing the long flight of centuries down we shall never find an era so replete with the wonderful as that in which we live, at this present. No! not when Semiramis flourished in all the pomp and splendour of a universal empress upon an Eastern throne; when the coronet of her fame encircled the terrestrial sphere and her luminous sceptre lit up the world, illuminating her constellation of empires. Not in the full blaze of Assyrian glory and strength, from Nimrod to Sardinapolis, extending over a period of nearly fifteen hundred years, have so many extraordinary events taken place as are concentred in the last half century. We live in an age of epochs— every year, every day, yea every moment, is an era within itself.

In reference to the question of slavery, it may be reasonably supposed that the Lord of light and life will not for ever slumber, he will not for ever see his children trodden down under the iron hoof of Southern despotism. Yes! and I would declare, had I the power, with the voice of Stentor, in the marketplace of a World's Metropolis, that the great Jehovah would prove himself a traitor to the sacred cause of truth and justice, did he for ever refuse to hear the cries of perishing millions! But hark!

> Jehovah thundering out of Zion,
> Thron'd between the cherubim,
> — *Milton*

may yet rain fiery hail upon this wicked land, as he did of old upon the cities of the Plains. Why are they oppressed? Napoleon Bonaparte says that "all men are born equal— science and talent alone can make a difference." Our most renowned orators and poets have sustained the assertion, and have ever been the champions of freedom.

> In the sight of our law, the slave-trader is a pirate and a felon, and in the sight of heaven an offender far beyond the ordinary depth of human guilt.
> — *Webster*

How is it possible that they, the slave-holders, can lie in peace when "darkness is over the face of the earth?" In the night time, alas!

> Nature's sweet restorer, balmy sleep,

that which Dr. Johnson calls

> The parenthesis of human woe,

and the great poet of the "Night Thought,"

> Sleep, great nature's second course,
> The balm of hurt minds,

can have no pleasures for them. The fact is, they have no consciences, or if they are possessed of any, they are made of brass or of adamant, on which no insertion may be made; or else, like India rubber, they stretch to all intents and purposes.

"Talk not to me" (says Lord Brougham) "of rights— talk not of the property of the planter in his slaves, I deny the right— I acknowledge not the property." Look to the old climes of Europe where for centuries unknown to history, monarchy and its twin brother despotism have reared their stronghold. We shall find slavery swept away even there, by almost all the rulers of all the kingdoms on that continent, occasioned more or less, no doubt, by

> the flood of British freedom, which, to the open Sea of the world's praise, from dark antiquity hath flowed.
> — *Wordsworth*

Such were the words of the sweet "Poet of the Lakes," and such, furthermore, was the language of the great Law Orator of Ireland:

> I speak in the spirit of British law, which makes liberty commensurate with, and inseparable from, British soil, which, proclaims even to the stranger and sojourner, the moment he sets foot on British earth, that the ground on which he treads, is holy and consecrated by the genius of universal emancipation.
> — *Curran*

I do not wish that my solitary opinion concerning slavery should be forced upon mankind. Not this, worse than feudal despotism, has met with execrations from the most splendid spirits, that ever adorned the world, and from the treasure house of memory I bring them forth, like an archangelic host, rallying at the command of some mighty leader, on the ethereal plains. But yet,

> I would not have a slave to till my ground;
> To carry me; to fan me while I sleep
> And tremble when I wake, for all the gold
> That sinews bought and sold, have ever earned:
> No! dear as freedom is, and in my heart's
> Just estimation, prized above all price,
> I'd much rather be myself the slave
> And wear the bonds, than fasten them on him.
> — *Cowper*

Sleep well, thou "amiable Poet," under thy monument at Olney.

Although thou didst not live to grace with thy lifetime our day, tens of thousands of hearts beat with the warmest affection to thy memory. Our eyes and the eyes of generations not yet conceived, down through countless ages, shall shed tears of gratitude at hearing thy blessed name, dear evangelical Bard whose fame shall ever be

By seraphs writ with beams of heavenly light.

When shall some mighty genius arise to fling a standard of light over the United States: when their own flag shall no longer be a subject for declamatory orators and punning poets.

UNITED STATES! Your banner wears two emblems— one of
fame;
Alas! the other that it bears reminds us of your shame:
The White Man's liberty, in types, stands blazing by your
Stars;
But what's the meaning of the stripes? they mean your
Negroes' scars.
— *Campbell*

Long before I had purchased myself from my owner I had a desire to visit Canada, although I had often heard many strange and romantic stories

Of that green land, cradled in the roar
Of western waves and wildernesses.
— *Revolt of Islam*

And I had already made up my mind

That a land of slaves shall ne'er be mine.
— *Byron*

So I went on my pilgrimage, where in times past as at the present, many

> A footstep was heard in the rustling brake,
> Where the cotton tree shadow'd the misty lake;
> And a murmuring voice, and a plunge from shore,
> And the slave was seen in the south no more.
> — *Longfellow*

And finally arrived in Toronto, Queen City of the West, where all may well exclaim in the language of the idolized bard of the "land of the heather and bell":

> Wha sae base as be a slave
> Let him turn and flee.
> — *Burns*

But, even here, I have met a prejudice equal to anything I ever experienced in the South. Thanks to the laws, it may go no further than verbal illustration! But the greatest prejudice of all is that against myself personally, held by people of my own colour, concerning that which they never had a chance of knowing the truth of, but which I have explained in the following pages to the satisfaction, I hope, of all enlightened and conscientious men.

It was to clear up my character, and do justice to humanity, that I was at first prompted to publish this pamphlet, for I was well aware that

> Slander lives upon succession,
> For ever housed where it once gets possession.
> — *Comedy of Errors*

And armed in the adamantine armour of conscious innocence and truth, I hope to repel the thrusts of

> Slander
> Whose edge is sharper than the sword,
> Whose tongue outvenoms all the worms of Nile.
> — *Cymbeline*

But it has been the lot of great men to be slandered. Clarkson and Wilberforce, who ranked high among the truly great and good of the world, in their day, were slandered. Time and the good sense of mankind are doing these illustrious philanthropists justice. So they will George Thompson, who was so recently assailed by the tongue of slander in our city, whilst ably and disinterestedly engaged in protesting against the wrongs inflicted upon my oppressed and injured African brethren, now held in bondage in the so-called "land of liberty"!

# Address to George Thompson, Esq. Member of the Imperial Parliament

His life was gentle, and the elements so mixed in him, that nature might stand up and say to all the world— this was a man.
—*Julius Caesar*

Long ages, may thy voice be sent
In anthems, loud and free,
From continent to continent;
Across from sea to sea.

Millions of hearts adore thy worth,
Yea, many nations bless
Thy name, renown'd through all the earth
As in this wilderness.

Advance with splendour and prevail
In thy triumphant course;
And distant ages yet may hail
Thee! second Wilberforce.

Still may thy mighty eloquence
Sweep on like western waves
Till opposition's banish'd, hence,
And freedom crown the slaves.

Long may'st thou stay to make us blest;
Display thy native charms:
Toronto, Queen of (all) the West,
Will clasp thee in her arms.

We love thee, in our hearts and souls,
For all thy virtues rare;
And while Ontario's water rolls
Thou shalt be mirror'd there.

This little work, with the exception of the quotations and a portion of the matter in the preface, is wholly original, containing a simple narrative of unvarnished facts, interspersed with such comments as I conceived to be necessary. I am led to make these remarks from the fact that I have seen a book for sale in this city purporting to be a production of Mr. Paola Brown, of Hamilton. The fact is, it is a copy, almost verbatim, of a book known as "Walker's Appeal," written by a coloured man of that name. In order to show the reader more plainly the diabolical attempt of Paola Brown to rob the memory of an estimable man of one of the boldest productions against slavery ever written and published in America, I will give the preface to a brief sketch of the life and character of David Walker, together with the sketch itself, written by Henry Highland Garnet, and published with the second edition of the book referred to in 1848. Hence it will be seen that Mr. Brown is not honest in putting forth a work like the one in question in his name and as his own production.

## Garnet's Preface to Walker's *Appeal*

Such is the very high esteem which is entertained for the memory of David Walker, and so general is the desire to preserve his *Appeal*, that the subscriber has undertaken and performed the task of re-publication, with a brief notice of his life, having procured permission from his widow, Mrs. Dewson.

The work is valuable, because it was among the first, and was actually the boldest and most direct appeal in behalf of freedom, which was made in the early part of the Anti-Slavery Reformation. When the history of the emancipation of the bondmen of America shall be written, whatever name shall be placed first on the list of heroes, that of the author of the *Appeal* will not be second.

*Troy, N.Y.*
*April 12, 1848*

## Garnet's Sketch of the Life and Character of David Walker

It is generally the desire of the reader of any intellectual production to know something of the character and the life of the author. The character of David Walker is indicated in his writings. In regard to his life, but a few materials can be gathered. What is known of him furnishes proof to the opinion which the friends of man have formed of him— that he possessed a noble and a courageous spirit, and that he was ardently attached to the cause of liberty.

Mr. Walker was born in Wilmington, North Carolina, September 28, 1795. His mother was a free woman, and his father was a slave. His innate hatred of slavery was very early developed. When yet a boy, he declared that the slave-holding South was not the place for him. His soul became so indignant at the wrongs which his father and his kindred bore, that he determined to find some portion of his country where he would see less to harrow up his soul. Said he, "If I remain in this bloody land, I will not live long. As true as God reigns, I will be avenged for the sorrow which my people have suffered. This is not the place for me— no, no. I must leave this part of the country. It will be a great trial for me to live on the same soil where so many men are in slavery; certainly I cannot remain where I must hear their chains continually and where I must encounter the insults of their hypocritical enslavers. Go I must."

The youthful Walker embraced his mother, and received a mother's blessings, and turned his back upon North Carolina. His father died a few months before his birth; and it is a remarkable coincidence that the son of the subject of this Memoir was also a posthumous child.

After leaving home, David Walker travelled rapidly towards the North, shaking off the dust of his feet, and breathing curses upon the system of human slavery, America's darling institution. As might be expected, he met with trials during his journey; and at last he reached Boston, Massachusetts, where he took up his permanent residence. There he applied himself to study, and soon learned to read and write, in order that he might contribute something to the cause of humanity. Mr. Walker, like most reformers, was a poor man— he lived poor, and died poor.

In 1827 he entered into the clothing business in Brattle Street, in which he prospered; and had it not been for his great liberality and hospitality, he would have become wealthy. In 1828, he married Miss Eliza ________. He was emphatically a self-made man, and he spent all his leisure moments in the cultivation of his mind. Before the Anti-Slavery Reformation had assumed a form, he was ardently engaged in the work. His hands were always open to contribute to the wants of the fugitive. His house was the shelter and the home of the poor and needy. Mr. Walker is known principally by his *Appeal*, but it was in his private works, and by his unceasing labours in the cause of freedom, that he has made his memory sacred.

With his overflowing heart, he published his *Appeal* in 1829. This little book produced more commotion among slave-holders than any volume of its size that was ever issued from an American press. They saw that it was a bold attack upon their idolatry, and that too by a black man who once lived among them. It was merely a smooth stone which this David took up, yet it terrified a host of Goliaths. When the fame of this book reached the South, the poor, cowardly, pusillanimous tyrants grew pale behind their cotton bags, and armed themselves to the teeth. They set watches to look after their happy and contented slaves. The Governor of Georgia wrote to the Hon. Harrison Grey Otis, the Mayor of Boston, requesting him to suppress the *Appeal*. His Honour replied to the Southern Censor, that he had no power nor disposition to hinder Mr. Walker from pursuing a lawful course in the utterance of his thoughts. A company of Georgia men then bound themselves by an oath, that they would eat as little as possible until they had killed the youthful author. They also offered a reward of a thousand dollars for his head, and ten times as much for the live Walker. His consort, with the solicitude of an affectionate wife, together with some friends, advised him to go to Canada, lest he should be abducted. Walker said that he had nothing to fear from such a pack of coward blood-hounds; but if he did go, he would hurl back such thunder across the Great Lakes that would cause them to tremble in their strongholds. Said he, "I will stand my ground. *Somebody must die in this cause.* I may be doomed to the stake and the fire, or to the scaffold tree, but it is not in me to falter if I can promote the work of emancipation." He did not leave the country, but was soon laid in the grave. It was the opinion of many that he was hurried out of life by the means of poison, but whether this was the case or not, the writer is not prepared to affirm.

He had many enemies, and not a few were his brethren whose cause he espoused. They said that he went too far, and was making trouble. So the Jews spoke of Moses. They valued the fleshpots of Egypt more than the milk and honey of Canaan. He died in 1830 in Bridge Street, at the hopeful and enthusiastic age of 34 years. His ruling passion blazed up in the hour of death, and threw an indescribable grandeur over the last dark scene. The heroic young man passed away without a struggle, and a few weeping friends

> Saw in death his eyelids close,
> Calmly, as to a night's repose,
> Like flowers at set of sun.

The personal appearance of Mr. Walker was prepossessing, being six feet in height, slender, and well proportioned. His hair was loose, and his complexion was dark. His son, the only child he left, is now 18 years of age, and is said to resemble his father; he now resides at Charlestown, Massachusetts, with his mother, Mrs. Dewson. Mr. Walker was a faithful member of the Methodist Church at Boston, whose pastor is the venerable father Snowden.

The reader thus has a brief notice of the life and character of David Walker.

Let no one suppose that I have written this for the sake of pecuniary gain. Such is not the case; but to defend myself against those who are not just enough to "render unto Caesar the things which are Caesar's." I have laboured night and day at my calling, therefore I have no need of charity at the hands of anyone. And from the proceeds of honest toil I have given away many pounds. Six pounds would not refund what I have given to fugitives during the last fall and winter. This I am prepared to prove.

*The Author*
*Toronto*
*July, 1851*

# A NARRATIVE OF THOMAS SMALLWOOD

I was born in Prince George's County, Maryland, the 22nd day of February, 1801. I was recorded to be set free at the age of thirty, in the clerk's office of that county. He who was instrumental in bringing it about was the Reverend J.B. Ferguson. Myself and sister had been bequeathed to the Lady whom he married and to her children. Although by the terms of the will he could not dispose of us at pleasure, yet by paying the amount at which we were valued he could do so by mutual agreement with those interested. That he did (for he was no friend to slavery) by paying $500 for me. With the amount he paid for my sister I never became acquainted. However, I served until I was thirty years of age, and my sister until she was twenty-five, so as to work out what he had paid for us. It is needless for me to go into a detail of the vicissitudes through which I passed during that period, more than to say, about five years before the time I was to be freed I hired myself from my master for the sum of $60 per year. About a year from that time I married. From then to the expiration of my servitude it was more than the joint labours of myself and wife could accomplish to pay my hire and to support ourselves and children. Hence it left me in debt at the end of my service $60, which I subsequently paid to the last farthing.

What little I know of the letter was obtained in the following manner, for I never had a day's schooling. The gentleman before mentioned, as my master, and his wife, learned me the English alphabet, and to spell in two syllables. When that became known to his neighbours they were amazed at the fact that a black or coloured person could learn the alphabet, yea, learn to spell in two syllables. I appeared to be a walking curiosity in the village where I then lived. When passing about the village I would be called into houses, and the neighbours collected around to hear me say the alphabet and to spell "baker" and "cider," to their great surprise (which were the first two words in the two syllables of Webster's *Spelling Book*). This may afford the reader a glimpse into the abyss of intellectual darkness into which the African race in America has been so long purposely confined, to serve the avarice and ends of their tyrannical oppressors. And to get out of which, by the aid of their friends, they are now struggling against many obstacles; prejudice on the part of the whites being among the most potent. But for my advancement from two syllables to the little I now possess I owe a deep debt of gratitude to a family of that people who are proverbial for their love of learning and imparting it to others, viz. Mr. John McLeod, a Scotch gentleman in whose excellent family I lived several years as servant. He had a large family of sons and daughters, these young gentlemen and ladies not only took great pleasure in learning me, but all the other servants about the house, who would take their teaching, for they were all coloured, and hired help notwithstanding.

He employed many servants about his house. He hired all. For be it said to his credit and humanity, he would own no slaves, although living in a slave-holding country. I have ever declined the many opportunities and offers I have had to become a tool in the hands of the enemies of that class of people with whom I am identified, and these, without regret on my part, deprived me of a considerable portion of this world's wealth. If my memory be not at fault, I was from the year 1822 or 1823, up to about 1830, an advocate of African Colonisation. I thought the object of that Society was the entire abolition of slavery in the United States; which I thought would lead to its final extinction everywhere else, thus placing my race, together with all others, in an elevated position. But I was greviously deceived. The object and policy of that Society proved to be, under the mask of philanthropy, the draining off the free coloured population from among the slave population by inducing them to emigrate to Africa. For the doctrine of its leaders was that the free population contaminated the slave population with a spirit of freedom, which made them uneasy in their bonds, and made it very difficult for their oppressors to hold them. But said they, "if we can get rid of the free negro population we can put a stop to any further emancipation, and thus have perpetual slavery without danger." This they sought to accomplish by various modes, one or two I will note.

First, by the influence of the African Colonisationists, it was decreed that no free coloured person should be employed on any of the government works in the United States, while, at the same time, they invited foreign emigration to supply their places. Thus, as much as possible, depriving them of a means of subsistence, in order to make them an easy prey to the wicked and insidious designs of the African Colonisation Society. Secondly, they had recourse to such of the coloured men who had acquired some influence over the minds of the free coloured people, among whom they lived, by holding out to them pecuniary inducements as a reward for their services in persuading and deluding their brethren into the African Colonisation trap. My humble self happened to be among the number to whom inducements were held out. And for the sake of my influence in that direction, I could have become a merchant in the Liberia trade, backed with the aid and influence of that Society. But I preferred to live in indigent circumstances, and enjoy my morsel with a good conscience, rather than be possessed with wealth and a burning conscience, with a recollection that I had come into possession of these through treachery to my afflicted race.

The slave-holders themselves can bear record that their gold and silver could not bribe me into a crusade against the interest of my brethren. And that while among them I bore an interminable hatred of their doings to them, and that I could not smother it, or else they would not have strove to entrap me as they did, and especially in 1843. I remember several occasions wherein I was concerned in secreting lots of fugitives who had been sold to the traders and fled to me that I might effect their escape, and the united rewards for whom, while I thus had them secreted, amounted from £200 to £250. These facts are so notorious that it is no hard matter for me to prove them in this city. But there were not found wanting those of my coloured brethren who became willing tools for the Colonisation Society. Among those who became so, and grew rich by it, was James Brown, and a Mr. McGill, the former had been a particular friend of mine, but in consequence of his connection with that Society we became opposed to each other and thus ended our friendship. My feeble efforts in the meantime were devoted to the anti-slavery cause, but the difficult question with me was what could I do to help to push forward so good a cause. I knew that I was in the midst of a slave-holding community, in which even the white man, who had more liberty and freedom of speech than I, dare not raise his voice in favour of freedom for the African's descendants in Christian America, although he might raise it as high as he pleased for the Greeks and Poles. I knew I could not go about the country and lecture against slavery, and that I could not call meetings to raise funds to help the poor way-worn fugitive toward the north star, seeking freedom from democratic and Christian slavery.

However, I determined to do something in the matter. Therefore I directed my efforts, first, against the influence of the Colonisation Society among coloured people, and by the assistance of the Lord I was in this successful. For where I lived, not one in a hundred could be induced to go to Africa. And so it was when I left. But how it is there now I cannot tell, for since the passage of the fugitive law, the Colonisationists are moving heaven and earth as it were to induce the free coloured people of the States to emigrate to Africa. The success of the fugitive bill may be attributed mainly to the influences of Northern Colonisationists. For anyone having any knowledge of that fraternity cannot but have observed that it is composed mostly of the great merchants, manufacturers, and aristocrats of the North, who suck their riches from the South, off from the sweat and blood of the African race, with as little reason and humanity as the stall-fed hog sucks the swill that is poured into his manger. These are they who lauded the Idol of Massachusetts, Daniel Webster, the great apostate, for the part he had taken in that infamous measure.

Secondly, to assist in the escape of all I could from slavery. After a time they crowded upon me by scores, and thank the Lord I was enabled to effect the escape of all except seven, who, through their own indiscretion and the treachery of others, I was foiled in effecting their escape. It is extremely hazardous to undertake to do anything for the slaves, but I do not blame them; it is just the way they are tutored in their raising. It is one of the grand policies of the slave-holders to keep up a continual lack of confidence of the coloured people toward each other, whether they be free or bond, by inspiring them with jealousy and envy against each other in order to keep down that sympathy and mutuality which is so necessary among people having a common interest at stake. Finally, it is the slave-holders' policy to keep their slaves in ignorance of everything except to know how to do their work and to act treacherously with each other. He or she that is the most expert at these, knowing nothing else, is, according to their language, the best negro. Hence it may be easily seen that the task of doing for them is a most dangerous one. Therefore much could not be done in the way of the underground railroad until 1842.

At that time, that most excellent and whole-souled Abolitionist, the Reverend C.T. Torry, made his appearance in Washington. I had heard of his arrest and trial at Anapolis, the seat of the Maryland government, to which place he had gone to take notes of the proceedings of the slave-holders then assembled in convention at that City, and I myself watched its progress with great anxiety. Although I was not at that time personally acquainted with him, yet immediately after his acquittal and return to Washington, the seat of the government of that Union, I formed an acquaintance with him through the agency of my wife, who took washing out of the house in which he then boarded. Through her, I sought and obtained an interview with him. And be it spoken to the praise of the lady with whom he boarded, that she and my wife were the only assistance we had for some time in the execution of our plans. At our first interview he informed me of a scheme he had in view, and requested my assistance, to which I readily assented. The scheme had for its object the rescue of a family of slaves, consisting of a man, his wife, and several children, who were owned by Mr. Bager of North Carolina, a Cabinet Minister, then living at Washington, and whose price for them was $1500. I was dispatched to see the woman and apprise her of the scheme, her husband being away North at the time begging money to pay for them. That good man thought that Mr. Bager had already got more of their labour than he was justly entitled to, according to the law of God. He therefore resolved if possible to deprive him of any pecuniary consideration for their liberty, in addition to the value of the labour he had already robbed them of. Besides, he was not in favour of paying slave-holders for any of their slaves that could be otherwise rescued from their grasp.

This the slave-holders and their pro-slavery apologists, yea, some who profess to look upon slavery with abhorrence, conceive to be monstrous, that the slave-holder should be deprived of his slaves without pay. Even the *Patriot* of this City, of the fourth of April, 1851, holds the following language in reference to it, "be thou just before you are generous." But they should also remember that justice has two sides, or in other words, a black side as well as a white side. And if it is just for slave-holders to compel men and women to work for them without pay, because they are *black*, and they have the power to do so; then it is equally just for them, or their friends, to deprive their masters of such labour without pay. Besides, the slave-holders are the aggressors. The African race never sold themselves to anyone, but they were stolen, and those who hold them in bondage are either the thieves or receivers, the one class being no better than the other and therefore the both are robbers. In common merchandise, if any are found with stolen goods in their possession, let them have come in possession of them ever so honestly on their part, yet are they deprived of such goods without a return of any part of the price that they paid for them. And if they cannot give a good account how they came by them, they are punished as the principal thief. And if a thief be taken with the spoil in his possession, it is rescued from him, and he punished according to law.

Now the slave-holders and dealers are robbers both of God and men. First, according to their own language, "all men are born free and equal, and are endowed by their creator with certain unalienable rights, among which are life, liberty, and the pursuit of happiness." Now the slave-dealers and -holders have robbed those they hold as slaves of those rights, and thereby robbed them of the happiness and pleasures flowing from the enjoyment of those rights. They have robbed God of that homage and praise due to him from beings with whom he has deposited those rights.

They have robbed the world of the benefit of the intellectual part that God designed they should perform in creation. The Algerines used to take the subjects of other nations and make slaves of them, and demand a price for their freedom. Some of the nations thus aggrieved gave them unmistakable proof that they would not submit to such injustice by sending against them some of their war ships to chastise them, and so put an end to it. So then, they who rescue those from the grasp of those who are continually robbing them are only performing the part of the good Samaritan, let slave-holders and their apologists say what they will. However, the man owned by Mr. Bager rejected (or was induced to do so through the influence of Colonisationists, and others in the North, who are always very anxious to recognise and acknowledge a right of property by man in man) the proposition of Mr. Torry, and so begged the money and paid for his family. If that money had been placed in the hands of Mr. Torry, he not only would have rescued that family but scores of others, who had as much claim on their misguided charity as that family had.

But this is only a small exhibition of their misdirected charity. I expected better things of Abolitionists, while I expected no good of Colonisationists. Notwithstanding these parties, without a murmur, would give their thousands to purchase a few individuals, they would complain bitterly against Mr. Torry and myself if they were called upon by us to give a few shillings to those fugitives whom we sent among them, to help them out of harm's way. And frequently some of those gangs charge us with taking an undue amount of money from them, and this brings me to notice the mode of our operations. Its foundation was that we had two places of deposit between Washington and Mason's and Dixon's line. The distance between Washington and the first was thirty-seven miles, the second was forty miles from the first. Over these our passengers generally travelled in two nights, and the third night they cross the line, and accomplish a distance of nine miles into Pennsylvania, to another place of deposit. And now I proceed to place the reader in possession of the mode of travel on the so-called underground railroad.

If we had women and children to convey, we had to hire conveyances at the rate of from $15 to $50 to the first place of deposit; the prices varied according to the numbers we had to convey. We had to pay teamsters a very high price in order to induce them to risk themselves and teams in so dangerous an enterprise. Besides, there was great difficulty in meeting with teamsters to whom we could make propositions of that kind. We have paid for the conveyance of one person fifteen dollars, for the conveyance of three, $25, and for eight or nine $50, for a distance of only thirty-seven miles.

I will relate one circumstance which took place during our operations which will serve to show how much justice there is in those charges before mentioned. About the latter part of August, 1842, the beloved friend, Torry, who is now no more, was about to leave Washington for the North, and I desired he would take with him about fifteen persons, men, women, and children. How that could be accomplished was a question of considerable importance. It was next to impossible to get a teamster to convey them at any price. The only alternative left was to purchase a conveyance. Then again, there was another obstacle in the way, almost insurmountable, which was the want of money. I got over this by the aid of a confidential friend who acted with me in all confidential matters relating to our operations, for though we had great difficulties to contend with, yet there were many things that worked in our favour.

There happened to be a huckster who had a waggon for sale that just suited our purpose, and for which he asked $53. The bargain was closed by paying the money. The next point of difficulty which lay in the way was to obtain a span of horses; this, however, was got over by our calling on a teamster to whom we had given $50 for one of those trips before alluded to, and who had a span for sale. Although not very good, they answered our purpose. We therefore agreed to give him $65 for them, paying $25 down and I and my friend becoming responsible for the balance, which was $40. Those obstructions were now overcome, yet still there were others in the way, though not quite so potent. We had to get a set of harness, and a pole made for the waggon, all which was to be done in one day. Until the morning of the day preceding the night on which Torry was to start with the fifteen, we had striven to hire a conveyance, but could not succeed. Notwithstanding, those persons had all been notified to meet at a certain place on that night, which notice could not be revoked. The people were on the spot at the appointed time. But we were not ready. Therefore we had to conceal them in various places in the city. In the meantime morning arrived, and with it a terrible uproar. One white family had no one to get breakfast; Ann had absconded taking with her all her children. Another had no one to black the boots, to set the table, and to wait breakfast; Bill had taken French leave, and gone about his business. A third had no one to drive the coach to church. Others were also in as bad a fix, hence a general pursuit was instituted on all the roads leading North, but all to no purpose, for the people were yet in the city.

One man, by name Gunnel, had a woman and two children whose husband desired to purchase them and for that purpose employed a gentleman to negotiate for them. But Gunnel insulted the gentlemen while he was trying to bargain for them, so he would have no more to do with the matter. The only alternative then left for the husband was to seek deliverance by flight, and for that purpose he with another man called on me to see what I could do for him in the matter. After telling his story, he stated to me the various difficulties he thought I would have to contend with— which to me were a mere moonshine— except the getting of a little girl, between five and six years of age. The child was required to sit all night by the side of a cradle in its master's and mistress' bed chamber, in order that if their child should awake, she should rock it, to prevent it from disturbing their slumbers. To get that child was the work of its mother, and to do it required some skill and caution. However, she did it admirably. As if by special providence of the Lord, a heavy sleep had come upon her master and mistress. She went into their bed chamber (as she informed me since) and took her child from the side of the cradle, without a stir on their part, never to be placed there again to spend a weary night for their comfort. She with her children arrived safe in

Canada, and she is now in Toronto. The husband of the woman told me that his wife's master frequently boasted that a nigger could not beat his time. I told him that if he would perform the part I had given him to do, by the assistance of the Lord, I would beat his time, though a nigger, according to his sense of the word. Thank the Lord, I did beat his time, and by the assistance of the Lord always could beat his and any of the rest of the slave-holders' time, but for the treachery of some of my own colour. He was on the six o'clock train of cars the next morning, for the North, and his satellites on every road leading North. He went as far as Baltimore but returned again on the evening train of the same day, not having got the least tidings of them, and no wonder for they had not left the city. But the beloved Torry started that same evening after the setting of the sun with fifteen persons, men, women, and children, for the North.

And here I must notice the remarkable interposition of the Lord in preserving them from capture. First, if we could have got ready they would have started the first night mentioned and the early pursuit which was made after them would have resulted in their capture; but on the contrary, notwithstanding our untiring perseverance we could not get ready. The result was their pursuers had gone a day ahead. And when they were going, some of their pursuers were returning on the same road, and but for another fortunate accident which happened they would have been met on the road and captured by them. Just as they came to a thick bush, within a convenient distance of the first place of deposit, the waggon, without exhibiting any previous weakness whatever, suddenly gave way and they had to turn aside into the bush. While they were thus snugly secreted in the bush, those who were hunting them passed by without seeing or hearing anything of them. This also served as an excellent delusion and put an end to all pursuit in that direction, for it was concluded they had gone by water. Mr. Torry then went to our first place of deposit, procured another waggon, and proceeded North with the people until he arrived at Troy, New York, without their owners hearing anything of them. I received a letter from him dated at that place containing these words in substance, "I have arrived at Troy safe with the chattels, and am now shipping them on board of a canal boat for Canada, and then I shall leave for Lynn, Massachusetts."

That feat having been accomplished, more satisfactorily to us than to the slave-holders, I turned my attention to laying plans for the performance of another that I accomplished in some three or four weeks. This was the sending off of twelve or thirteen slaves, to the great annoyance of the slave-holders. Notwithstanding there was a terrible uproar about that place, and a reward of $2000 offered for the detection of the person or persons who were thus depriving them of their goods and chattels, I continued to defy detection, and sent them off in gangs of never less than a dozen. I frequently had lots of slaves concealed about in Washington, who had fled to me for safety when they got wind that their masters were about to sell them to the slave-traders. The united rewards for them would amount to between $600 and $800 and $1000. These then were the times if I was a traitor to my brethren, with which my enemies have attempted to brand me, when I could have made my jack. It is passing strange, and not to be credited by any reasonable, just, and unprejudiced person, that I should, for a paltry sum of a few dollars or pounds, become an enemy to my brethren for whom I have almost worn myself out. While those who have had the audacity to accuse me (who have stood in the midst of dangers for my race, beset on every side by enemies), stand off at a respectful distance, out of harm's way, and like cowardly curs bark at slave-holders, but do nothing more. On the contrary, I employed persons and furnished them with the means to purchase food for them until a convenient time should arrive for their departure, and then I would pack them off.

For several reasons, the entire arrangement, management, and setting off those gangs forward, I had to attend to myself. It was not practicable for me to travel with them always, because suspicion had already pointed to me, and I could not even be absent from Washington without its being known. Therefore my absence at the times of the departure of those gangs might have led to my arrest, and an investigation have resulted in my conviction. Besides, I was the sole proprietor of the so-called underground railroad in that section, it having been started without the assistance of any earthly being save Torry, myself, my wife, and the lady with whom he boarded. Torry having gone North, the burden and responsibility of consequences rested entirely on me, therefore I had to watch every moment as with an eagle's eye. I generally went out on the suburbs of the city previous to the night intended for their departure and selected the place at which they were to assemble, never selecting the same place a second time; nor were more than two allowed to come in company to the place selected, and that in different directions, according to the advice of Mr. Torry.

I had at one time two more persons, in addition to the good friend Torry already mentioned, acting with me. Had I been a physiognomist, I might have been more fortunate in my selection, but not being acquainted with that science I was left to the mercy of every scoundrel who chose to feign himself a friend, hence the last mentioned individuals proved themselves to be polished villains.

One of them, by name George Lee, was appointed to conduct the people to the first place of deposit, and there give them into the care of a friend, who was to take them off his hands and conduct them about forty miles further and then give them in charge of another. Lee turned out to be both swindler and traitor for he went about among the slaves collecting money in my name from them, appropriating it to his own use, telling them that I would send them off at such and such times, without my having any knowledge of the fact. At length some of them became impatient and came to me and informed me that they had paid him sums of money with an understanding that I was to send them off. Some of these I had before his face and he could not deny the fact. Hence his villainy having been exposed, and he knowing that he had lost my confidence, he went on from one degree of rascality to another till he committed an act the perpetration of which wounded my feelings more severely than anything that had ever happened to me, and which shewed a degree of ungratefulness and unreasonableness on the part of a man whose wife and two children I had so recently been instrumental in rescuing from the grasp of that boasting slave-holder, Bill Gunnel, whose watchword was that a nigger could not beat his time. That actually surpassed anything I ever met with.

There were two men out on a scout, hiding and dodging from their owners. A friend of theirs came to me and requested I would try and get them off. I could not hold out to him much prospect of my being able to get them away inasmuch as through the treachery of some of our brethren the way was so completely hedged up that it was impossible to get anyone away at that time. I promised him to do what I could. He then placed in my hands, for their use, a small sum of money while he kept the men concealed under his care. George Lee was a half-brother to this friend of theirs, and he, learning that I had the money, and wishing to get it for his own use, went to his brother, who was anxious to get them off, and pretended he would get them away safe if he would let him have the money I had got, when in fact he knew he could do no such thing. However, the friend of the men came to me, got the money, and gave it to Lee, his half-brother, who instead of getting them off safe took the poor creatures to the man whose wife and two children had gotten off, and who was coachman for a gentleman in that city, and got him to take and conceal them in his stable loft, and feed them at his own expense, while Lee made use of their money, making him believe, at the same time, that I had it. Of all this I was in total ignorance except the giving up the money, notwithstanding it was whispereed about by the man, that he had the men, and was feeding them at his own expense, and I had their money and would do nothing for them. Now George Lee, without doubt, wishing to get out of this piece of rascality without myself or anyone else knowing the game he had played, determined to betray the men into the hands of their masters. This, doubtless, he did by informing the slave-catchers where they were. For a part of the very conversation the man had with Lee the day previous, as repeated to him by the slave-catchers at the time they took the men out of his stable loft; and notwithstanding this, and the part I had taken in the escape of his wife and two children, together with many others, he charged me with betraying them.

I mention this with no unkind feeling towards him, or to wound his feelings, nor to revive old feuds. But it is necessary, because I afterwards received information from a friend which led me to believe that he was labouring under an erroneous impression that I still had those men's money, and that I had betrayed them for the same reasons which really had induced George Lee to do it. I therefore requested the man to whom I had returned the money, and my friend from whom I had received that information, together with the man, and Lee, to meet at my house without letting them know what my object was. They all met, and I then requested the friend of those men, who was as before stated half-brother to Lee, to say if I had or had not returned to him the money I had received from him for the benefit of his friends. He said, "You did." The man then asked him what he had done with it. He said, "I gave it to George Lee." He then asked Lee what he had done with it. He, with considerable confusion, acknowledged he had appropriated it to his own use. Here then was a complete solution of the villainous game he had been playing. The same man also at that meeting wanted to know of Lee what he had done with some $50 or $60 which he had collected from slaves, and put in his possession, for the purpose of conveying them away. This it seems he had also appropriated to his own use. This also led me into the light of something I had not before known.

Now the fact is that there was not a coloured man to be found about there, who thought enough about the condition of his race to make it a matter of study how he might assist to ameliorate their condition, or one who had the courage to try to do anything for them. Yet, after I, who had made it a matter of study for years, had by the assistance of the Lord and Mr. Torry opened a way through which scores were successful in their attempt to escape from slavery, there were plenty of champions of my own colour, who for the sake of filthy lucre attempted to build upon the foundation I had laid. It appeared that that man, as others, thought that I was acting in what I was doing as agent for the Abolitionists. Hence for the purpose of supplanting me, they commenced a correspondence with my friend G. in Baltimore, who acted the same part there that I did in Washington. But he would not listen to their false representations because he knew it to be an underhanded piece of business on their part, and that men guilty of such treachery could not be trusted with such ticklish operations. Besides they might have known (if my colour there could have been trusted with such secrets) that I was the establisher of that underground railroad, and that I was as independent of the Abolitionists in my operations as oil is of water, with one or two exceptions. And with regard to pecuniary aid offered me by them it was not the amount of one farthing. But with this drama my troubles did not end, for they proceeded against me from one degree of rascality to another trying to entrap me, and at the same time to appear innocent of the deed. But I was aware of their stratagems and was by the assistance of the Lord enabled as it were to escape by the skin of my teeth.

I will proceed to notice another remarkable piece of treachery, perpetrated by Benjamin Lannum. I had seen a reward offered in the papers for the apprehension of a slave who had absconded from his owner, taking with him a considerable amount of money, doubtless his own earnings. This man lingered about the neighbourhood of his owner, unable to effect his escape, till at length hearing of me he employed a man, by the name of Franklin, who came about twenty-five miles to obtain my assistance in effecting his escape. With a great deal of reluctance, owing to the difficulties which lay in the way through treachery, I consented, after charging him not to bring any but the man and two others whom he said he wished me to take. He was particularly cautioned to bring no females, because the difficulties to be encountered made it impracticable to have any with me. Besides, it was only the precarious situation of the first mentioned man that had more weight with me than the dangers with which I had to contend in effecting his escape.

I appointed the time and place at which Franklin was to meet me, with the three men, which was at eight o'clock, on the succeeding Saturday night, at the shore of the eastern branch of the Potomac, opposite to Washington. I then engaged a confidential friend, whom I shall ever hold in grateful remembrance for his fidelity, to accompany me in a boat to the place above mentioned. Franklin met us there, but not according to agreement with regard to time, nor to the persons he was to bring. For instead of eight o'clock, he did not arrive till twelve; and then he brought only two men and a woman; leaving behind the very man whose case induced me to undertake the enterprise. Eight o'clock had been chosen in order to give time to reach the city and have the people concealed before the ringing of the bell for ten o'clock, at which time every coloured person, no matter how respectable, had to be indoors; or, if taken, be carried to the lock-up house, and next morning, if free, pay a fine of $5 or go to the workhouse; if a slave, the master to pay a fine of $5 or the slave receive as many lashes on the bare back. However, being thus belated, I so managed as to reach the city by four o'clock in the morning, it being between daybreak and daylight, at which time the watch retired from the duties of the night. I had given notice to Benjamin Lannum of what was going on because he was the person who had attended to the fugitives that I had concealed from time to time. I, therefore, on reaching the city, proceeded with the people in the direction of the place where I intended to conceal them, calling at the dwelling of Lannum on my way. After giving proper directions relative to the men and woman, I gave them into his charge, and retired to my home after being out all the night.

On reaching home I found Franklin there. I pressed upon him the absolute necessity laid on him to bring the man he had left behind within my reach, because his case was almost desperate. Besides, he had received $25 of that man's money, for services which would not be performed until he brought the man to me. I had discovered also that the men whom Franklin brought, had, by some means or other, possessed themselves of all the man's money, and were desirous of making their escape to the North, leaving him to his fate, whatever that might be, so that they might have the money for themselves.

I cannot but believe that Franklin was privy to that infamous design, which I was determined not to be a party to, if possible, to carry out. I told Franklin that I would wait until the following Wednesday, so as to give him ample time to find the man if he was disposed so to do. In the meantime I intended to go as far as Baltimore and acquaint my friend G. of what was doing, and to obtain his assistance when I should arrive in that city with the fugitives; and then return to Washington and start with the people for the North, on the Wednesday night before mentioned. But all my designs were frustrated, through treachery, and myself like to have been entrapped.

Franklin, after taking breakfast at my table, started for home, and after crossing the river and proceeding about two miles met the man. Notwithstanding he had received $25 for his services, he would not return to me with him until the poor fellow had agreed to give him $20 more, which I paid to him, on his return to me with the man, out of $150 that had been placed in my hands by one of the first two men he had brought, for the expense of the jaunt. He brought the man to my house the same day, which was sabbath, about eleven o'clock, and it being church-going time of the day they were not noticed more than other persons. I kept him at my house until near six o'clock, because at that hour crowds would be again going to the churches, and he could pass to the place where the others were concealed, without being much observed. For that purpose I sent my good friend who had assisted me across the river with the others, to Lannum, about six o'clock, to inform him that the man left behind had come, and that I wished him concealed with the others. To my great surprise and consternation he returned to me with the information that the fugitives had been taken by Williams, the slave-trader, soon after they had been concealed, which was early in the morning.

Notwithstanding this, Lannum never gave me information of the fact until I sent my friend to him, about six o'clock, for the object above mentioned, which, with other circumstances, proved that Lannum gave Williams information of their whereabouts. Besides, it was said that a woman saw him go towards Williams' dwelling, saw also a window hoisted, and a conversation held between him and Williams. Of this the woman upbraided him at a chapel the same day. Not only so, without suspicion on my part yet with some surprise, it was not over an hour after I had parted from him and the fugitives before he was at my house for the money I had agreed to give him for taking care of them until I got them away. The amount I gave him was $30. This sum may seem large to those unacquainted with such operations, but for that want of sympathy with each other that exists among us, I, on various occasions, had to pay some of them considerable sums to get them to act on behalf of our suffering brethren. This was a case in point, though it did not prevent treachery.

Fortunately for myself, the persons thus betrayed by Lannum could not describe me to the slave-catchers, for I was only with them in the dark, although they could call my name. Yet as there were other Smallwoods in Washington, they could not find the guilty one, therefore I escaped the snare laid for me in that piece of treason. Lannum, of course, through policy, did not point me out, for he tried very hard to have me believe he was not guilty of the crime, and indeed I dared not charge it home to him. For I was, as I had been for some time, between two fires. My own colour, on the one hand, through envy and for the sake of filthy lucre, were trying to betray me; while on the other hand, the slave-holders were offering large rewards for the detection of the person or persons who were thus robbing them of their goods and chattels.

There was another circumstance which aggravated my precarious position, among some of my colour. I had a controversy with a coloured man, a preacher, by name Abraham Cole, growing out of a rebuke I gave him in a leaders' meeting, in consequence of his improper talk. Consequently his friends strove to do me all the injury they could by making use of the most disreputable means to accomplish their object. They would try to make it appear among the respectable portion of my own colour, that I was a great traitor to my race, by circulating the most absurd falsehoods about me; while on the other hand, they would try underhandedly to point me out to the slave-holders as being the man who was aiding in the escape of their slaves. By the assistance of the Lord I so far evaded all the snares set for me. But the scene of difficulties did not end with these. Seeing that through the treachery of some of my colour I could be of no further service to my poor slave brethren, and that the cloud of treachery began to thicken, and get blacker and blacker over me, and that Washington was no longer a place of safety for me, I determined to seek a resting place in some other clime. I was convinced that the place could only be found in America, to my satisfaction, in the British dominions, where the laws are equal, and know no difference between man and man on account of colour.

Therefore, to accomplish that object, I set out from Washington, on the 30th of June, 1843. I passed rapidly on my journey without stopping to hold any parley with Abolitionists or anyone else, except in Philadelphia and Albany, to explain away some falsehoods left at those places by miscreant fugitives, and which, as usual, were too eagerly swallowed by some Abolitionists. On the fourth day of July I arrived at Toronto, in Canada; and how different were my feelings that day to what they would have been had I been in the States. There I would have been compelled painfully to witness as I had done for many years their hypocritical demonstrations in honour of a day, which they say, brought to them freedom. But I sorrowfully knew that it was in honour of a day that brought to me, and my race among them, the most degrading, tyrannical, and soul-withering bondage that ever disgraced the world or a nation. But here, I was on Canada's free soil, and I may rejoice and give thanks to God in honour of that day, it being the day on which I first put my feet in a land of true freedom, and equal laws. Having visited several places in Canada, I speedily returned to Washington, there to have another contest with slave-holders, and treacherous coloured persons, and prepare to take leave of that mock metropolis of freedom, and sink of iniquity.

On arriving there, I learned that it was rumoured about that I was the person that was getting away the slaves and that my visit to the North was to make arrangements to further that object. I found it therefore necessary to make speedy arrangements for leaving. In consequence of false information having been given by James Williams, a slave, to Charles Miller, a butcher, to the effect that I was about to leave for Canada and take with me a number of slaves— among whom, a woman belonging to the said Charles Miller— my house was surrounded early on the night preceding the morning I was to start with my family by the watch, and Goddard, their Captain at their head. I was seated in the front door when a policeman with whom I was acquainted came to me and said, "Thomas, I have been instructed, in consequence of information, that you intend starting for Canada with some slaves, to come and search your house." I invited him to do so. After doing so he left the inside of the house but did not leave the premises until searching the house a second and third time, the last of which the blackguard Goddard came in and said, "Smallwood, I understand you are going off to Canada and intend to take slaves with you." He then proceeded to examine those in the house as to whether they were chattels or free negroes. There were ten or twelve persons present in the house at the time preparing to leave for Canada the next morning, and take a final leave of such beautiful scenes of republican freedom. It is true that I had another slave woman concealed in my house and for whom I for some time had been trying to make a way of escape. But I had no intention of taking this woman or any other slaves with me, for I had made arrangements with confidential friends to take and keep her until a way of escape could be made. But to get her out of the house unperceived was a matter of great importance. However, that was speedily accomplished by some females, who took her through a back door into the garden, and concealed her in some corn.

On the third day of October, 1843, with considerable difficulty, I got my family on board the steamboat Columbia, for Baltimore; intending myself to remain in Washington that day, to dispose of some furniture at auction, and then take the cars the next morning for that city, which would have conveyed me there at the same hour the steamboat arrived. But I was assailed on my way down to the boat with my family, by two constables and an Irishman of the name of Kennedy. A relative of George Lee lived with Kennedy, to whom Lee had revealed all my operations, and he revealed the same to Kennedy. Therefore he could tell me as much about my operations as if he had witnessed them personally. His object was, however, to obtain from me $29 and some cents, the amount of a note which I had endorsed to take a man out of gaol, but which was not due for some time. I paid it. Kennedy intimated at the same time that I ought to pay a certain amount to prevent my being arrested on the charges preferred against me. The constables however declined to arrest me then, saying they had no warrant to do it. But I was aware that if I returned to the house to get the furniture I had left to dispose of at auction as I had intended, I would be arrested through the information given by Kennedy. I therefore instead of returning sought a place of concealment for that day. About four o'clock the next morning I set out on foot, on a by-road, for Baltimore, not daring to attempt a passage on the cars. I doubted not that the constables were looking out for me, they doubtless having had knowledge of my original design to take the cars that morning. I would have set out earlier, but my place of concealment was within the limits of the city, and I did not think it safe to start until four in the morning, that being the time the watch retired from duty.

I reached Baltimore at five o'clock the same day and found my wife and children. She had undergone much uneasiness on my account, notwithstanding she had sufficient presence of mind to make arrangements to remove the only obstacle that lay in the way of our obtaining a speedy passage out of Baltimore, the last place of danger to me. The time had been that it was only necessary for a coloured person to present a paper purporting to come from the office of the county clerk, having the seal of the said county stamped on it, and a description of the person, certifying the bearer to be a free negro, to obtain a conveyance on any of the public highways. But at that time it was not so, in consequence of several instances of stage and steamboat proprietors being sued for the value of slaves that were proved to have absconded on their conveyances. Hence to anticipate any contingencies in that way, the proprietors of public conveyances in the Slave States required coloured persons presenting themselves for a passage to procure a responsible person or persons to enter bond to the amount of the value of the person or persons wishing to procure a passage. By the time therefore that I had reached Baltimore my wife had gotten over that difficulty through the kindness of Mr. Pitman, an excellent gentleman of English parents, who signed a bond to the amount of $2000 as the value of myself and family. I had forwarded a letter to some friends in Albany, New York, informing them of my condition, and letting them know that I was separated from my wife and children, and the probability was that I should not be able to join them before reaching Philadelphia or New York, and that they were short of money.

Leaving Baltimore, Thursday evening, seven o'clock, we reached Albany about twelve o'clock, Saturday, and found that those friends to whom I wrote had employed a man to meet my family, and to take charge of them; a kindness on their part I shall ever hold in grateful remembrance, especially Messrs. Croker, Thomson, and Latimore, of Albany, New York. I mention these because of their unbounded benevolence to fugitives falling in their way. There are other bright stars of benevolence in that city, the names of whom are too numerous to mention. Notwithstanding their kind offers to assist me in business, I declined to settle there. I pushed on for Canada, and arrived at Toronto, October 14, 1843, and settled in it, and I have never regretted one moment having carried out my first intention. Inasmuch as I had to leave the metropolis of the United States to seek freedom, from whose legislative halls freedom is proclaimed to all the world, except to the African race, I would seek it in no part of that inconsistent nation, because I was aware that there was no freedom for a coloured person within its limits. I was only a few days in Toronto, before I was solicited by four men, Osburn Turner, James Woodland, Stephen Brown, and Levi Scott (the last three were a part of some of the gangs gotten away by me from Washington) to try and get their wives and children, who were in Washington, to them. I consented to do so, and for that object I got up a subscription list, and started for the States, and after trudging about Western New York three weeks, I reached Albany, only having obtained about $40, for I found the Abolitionists more willing to give their thousands to a defunct institution, got up by a few designing persons in the name of coloured refugees in Canada, but in reality, I believe, to line their own pockets, than to give a few shillings to get those families to their husbands. The coloured people, as a body, in Canada, will never appreciate the benevolence, if benevolence it may be called, of those who gave large sums of money and quantities of clothing in their name, and that against their will, to enrich those who constituted themselves the managers therein.

I had written to Mr. Torry about four weeks previous to my arrival in Albany, informing him that I was trying to collect money, and for what object, requesting him at the same time to forward a letter to a certain friend in Washington, desiring him to send the above mentioned families to Philadelphia. This he did, but he had also conceived the following scheme, that we should try and obtain a team and proceed to Washington, and bring away as many slaves as we could. For the accomplishment of that I was furnished with a second subscription list (having given the first together with the money collected into the hands of Mr. Torry) with which I spent another week trying to collect more money for the furtherance of the enterprise we had in view, but with poor success. In the meantime however, thirty dollars were sent to Mr. Torry from Vermont, to be applied in trying to get the wife and child of James Baker, a young man whose escape we had effected, and whose good conduct had won for him the good wishes of some of the good people of that State. With this, and that which I had collected, we departed on a certain Friday evening from Albany, for New York City, and arrived there on Saturday morning. Thence we proceeded to Philadelphia, arriving there on the evening of the same day, and stayed there over Sunday.

One circumstance I ought to have mentioned in connection with Lannum's treachery, previously mentioned, I notice here. William Nichols, a preacher of the African Methodist Episcopal Church, was sick on his death bed (though he did not, I presume, suppose himself so near death's door), and I called to see him. While there I communicated to him some of the circumstances connected with the capture of those people, which he twisted into a wicked falsehood, and as I have been informed, died with it on his lips, that I betrayed those persons. That lie was the only testimony he left of his acceptance with God; a poor one indeed. Therefore, on arriving in Philadelphia, I met with the outrageous falsehood for the first time. Mr. Paine, a preacher of the same denomination as Nichols, and at that time stationed at Washington, became the devil's pack-horse, and bore the falsehood to that city.

On that Monday we started for Wilmington, Delaware, arrived there the same day, and put up at that excellent gentleman's, Mr. Thomas Garrot's. The next day, Tuesday, we put out for Gannet's Square, in Pennsylvania. There we obtained a waggon and span of horses and proceeded the same day for Maryland, and in the night of the same day reached a tavern near Mason's and Dixon's line, and put up for the night. Early the next morning we were off again for Baltimore, and after driving all day and late at night, we arrived in Baltimore at about eleven o'clock. The next morning we expected the four families we had written for. I therefore set out in pursuit of them in the direction of the dock, where the steamboat from Washington lay, and met two of them, the other two having declined to come. After making the necessary arrangements for their departure to Philadelphia, we again started for Washington at two o'clock the same day, and arrived there at eleven o'clock the same night, and stopped at friend John Bush's, who had, according to our request, made the necessary arrangements for carrying out the enterprise. We kept ourselves very close the next day, intending to start at night with our chattels, about fourteen in number. Unfortunately for us the police of that city had been made aware of our coming, therefore while I was harnessing the horses in the stable, and Mr. Torry was storing the people in the waggon, a friend came to me and said, "friend Smallwood, I see some white men standing out there on the hillside and they look like constables." I immediately communicated the same to Mr. Torry, who said to me, "I will go and see." He soon returned to me trembling, saying they were constables, and requested me to try and get the people out of the waggon. They were ten in number; but he soon said to me, "You can't, they are closing on us." Therefore we had to make speed in making our own escape and leave the poor creatures to the mercy of the bloodhounds.

After getting about a quarter of a mile from the place, I heard the clanking of the chains, and shrieks of the poor souls, but we could afford them no help, they were in the claws of the lions. Mr. Torry and myself became separated from each other during our flight. In the meantime, I fell in with a particular friend, who said to me, "Go home with me and stay and rest yourself until tomorrow night, and then start." But I thanked him and declined his kind offer, and told him I would not stop until I reached Baltimore, for that while they would be ransacking Washington thinking I was still there, I would be far away out of their reach. So I took leave of him just as the bell began to ring for ten o'clock, at which time all coloured persons had to be indoors, and pushed forward for Baltimore, steering clear of every dwelling on the road by taking a circuitous route, fearing that the dogs might be roused, and that they might rouse the inmates, and I myself be attacked for a fugitive. For I knew that if I was, I should be lodged in gaol for a fugitive, and my case would be hazardous. For I had left my free papers at home in Toronto, not thinking when I left that I should go into any of the Slave States; and they were not then required in any of the so-called free states. However, I reached Baltimore the next morning, Saturday, about eight o'clock, and kept a close house at my friend G.'s until that day week.

Mr. Torry did not come for three or four days after the catastrophe, but remained in Washington to make arrangements with Mr. Hall, a lawyer for the defence of our friend John Bush, from whose premises we were routed, and the people taken; for which he was arrested. Monday morning, being the first issue of the Baltimore *Sun* after its editor had information of the affair, it contained a detailed account of the matter, from a correspondent in Washington, to the following effect,

> Information having been received by the police of this city, that a negro fellow by the name of Thomas Smallwood, who had removed to Toronto, Canada, a few months ago, and a white man, arrived in this city on Thursday night, about eleven o'clock, with a team, for the purpose of taking away a number of slaves; a strict

> look out was kept, and on Friday night the waggon with the horses and a number of slaves were taken, but Smallwood is not yet captured.

This shewed me, as I had anticipated, that they were on the wrong scent, and that while they were beating the air and moving heaven and earth as it were to find and arrest me in Washington, I, by the assistance of the Lord, was far away out of their reach. Mr. Torry was not molested during his stay in Washington. Being a white man they dared not publish him, or bring any charge against him, because they were not sure that they could sustain it; and it would only have subjected them to legal action. But with regard to myself it was different. I was a coloured man, and so it made no difference; besides, they had other charges against me which they could sustain.

Mr. Torry arrived in Baltimore from Washington the succeeding week, and afforded me the means to reach Philadelphia, for I had none, having delivered all I collected into his hands except what little I expended while collecting. On the Saturday evening following the one on which I arrived in Baltimore I set out for Port Deposit, about forty miles from Baltimore, in company with my friend G. and a slave man, who was to accompany me to Philadelphia. Friend G. had to accompany me, as he did fugitives from slavery, because I had been published as a fugitive from justice, and was liable to be taken and carried back to Washington, where I should be tried, and if convicted, sent to the Penitentiary for fourteen years. Not only so, that was his part in the transaction of the underground railroad, and with him I was unacquainted. A little south of Port Deposit bridge, on the road side, lived a woman whose name was Turner. This woman had been in the habit of keeping fugitives for friend G. until friend P. from the other side, who kept a secret ferry, would come and take them, and conduct them, on his part of the road, into Pennsylvania, and deliver them to the protection of the Quakers. But she had turned traitress and had betrayed some into the hands of their owners, therefore it was necessary to keep clear of her. In order to do this we thought to pass her house before daylight, so as not to be seen. But when we got opposite the house, to our surprise, who should be standing at the window looking down on us but the old dame herself; she being so used to friend G.'s movements, it was hard to delude her.

We passed on, however, and crossed the bridge just at the rising of the sun, and went to friend P.'s, and there put up for the day. We remained there until six o'clock in the evening, at which time the house was beset by constables from that den of slave-catchers, Habertigrass, a village near Mason's and Dixon's line. They were doubtless made acquainted with our whereabouts by Mrs. Turner, who knew as well as we did, where we stopped. The slave who was with us, at their first approach, went out of the house into the road, whom they interrogated as to who he was, and where he was from, and then made a rush in the house, evidently in search of me. As the house stood at the foot of a mountain, and had several rooms in it, I, while they were searching one, slipped through a secret door, which had been put there for such purposes, and was soon lost to them in the thick bush that covered the hill. There was considerable snow on the ground, it being December, but I went on all night trudging through the snow, up hill and down hill, over streams and through plains in a part of the country I knew nothing of. My object, of course, was to reach Pennsylvania, and at about three o'clock in the morning I thought I might be in that State. Therefore I ventured to hail the inmates of a small house on the roadside and inquired what county I was in, and if there were any coloured people living in that vicinity, for I did not wish to be thought a fugitive by inquiring whether I was in Pennsylvania or not. However, the answer satisfied me that I was in that State; it also informed me that opposite there lived two coloured families whose houses I could see through a little skirt of bush that intervened, so I bore away for them. Passing by the first, I rapped at the door of the second, and after answering to the call, "Who is that?" and telling my story, the door was opened and I received a hearty welcome.

I was not long in the house before I let them know that I wanted something more than being let in, warmed by two fires, one in a stove, and one in a chimney or fireplace, between which I had snugged myself. I had eaten nothing since the previous morning, and of that I very quickly let them know. The daughter of Ezekiel Clark (for that was the name of the good man of the house)— a handy good-looking young woman— cheerfully arose from her bed and ministered to my necessity. I learned there that the nearest railroad depot for Philadelphia was fourteen miles, so after being prevailed on to take a little more to eat, I set out about nine o'clock for that place to take the cars for Philadelphia, and reached it a little before six in the afternoon. Taking the cars at six o'clock I was in Philadelphia by nine o'clock the same evening. After spending one day there, during which I occupied my time in listening to the debates in an anti-slavery convention then assembled in that city, the anti-slavery committee received a despatch from Mr. Torry,* urging that I should leave immediately for other parts of the North; that the slave-holders were in hot pursuit of me. Therefore I took passage on board of a steamer for Albany, New York, on my way to Canada. The reader may remember that we met two of the four families spoken of in a preceding part of this narrative, whom we sent to Philadelphia, to remain until we returned. They also accompanied me, but as none of us had any money with which to travel, though I was known, they were not, the anti-slavery committee anticipating that they would have difficulty in raising means to get along, furnished the females with a paper, purporting that they were fugitives from bond slavery, whereas they were not, but which delusion I was not at liberty to dispel. So we travelled on slowly, getting a little here and there, and to make up the deficiency I made use of what little I had, which was only six dollars, that had been given to me for my own use. Our means not being sufficient, I sold my watch in Buffalo to get them to Toronto, which city we reached on the 23rd of December, 1843, in the steamer *Transit*. I mention the steamer, because Captain Richardson, according to his usual benevolence, reduced the fare for us.

Now with regard to the advantages that would accrue to the coloured people if they settled in Canada, politically and domestically, they have been kept in total ignorance, and our abolition friends on the other side have contributed not a little to that ignorance. I would be greatly annoyed when with great danger to my own freedom I had got off slaves and advised them to go to Canada, to hear when they had got North they had been induced by the Abolitionists not to go to Canada. They told them the most absurd stories about it imaginable, and promised them perfect freedom and safety in the Northern States; whereas they knew they could do no such thing. Added to that, many persons of my own colour came to Canada, and because they could not live in idleness and laziness, returned to the States, and made unfavourable reports about Canada. These tales were eagerly swallowed by others of my own colour in the States, as being true, instead of coming to see for themselves. Now, as a general rule, there can be no better evidence of the worthlessness of coloured people than when they leave Canada and go to the States, and give it a bad name, and say they cannot live in it. It is a remarkable fact, of which our white fellow subjects have not been idle observers, that hitherto the coloured population of Canada, in the general, have been an industrious and sober class of people. And this is owing to the circumstance that when any worthless and idle ones came to Canada, they found no encouragement for their lazy and idle habits; hence they make back tracks for the States, and I pray God that none such may ever find a resting place in Canada. But on the other hand, I would say to every sober, industrious coloured man in the States, come to Canada, and you will get freedom, yea British freedom! Which is the best national freedom in the world! But the policy which has been pursued by our abolition friends in persuading the fugitives to settle in the northern states has been attended with the most disastrous consequences. They appealed to the hopes and fears of the poor fugitives, and made them believe that Canada was one of the most frightful spots on the globe. By this means thousands were induced to settle in the Northern States who have now by the passage of the iniquitous fugitive law to break up, sacrifice what little they had accumulated, and fly to Canada, and begin anew.

Whereas if they had been encouraged, or even let alone, they would have gone to Canada at first, and be now secure in their persons and property as British subjects. Besides, another consequence growing out of that policy was that the great accumulation of fugitives in the Northern States was a great annoyance to the slave-holders, who, coming North annually, would either see or hear of their own or neighbours' slaves, who had escaped from them, but whom they could not conveniently capture. But at length, knowing their power and influence over the North, they determined to have a law by which they could make their northern vassals the captors of their fugitives. Now, if that accumulation had been in Canada, I opine that there could have been no wish for that law on the part of slave-holders, and certainly not on the part of others, knowing that it could have no effect on any part of the glorious empire of Britain. I do not wish however to attribute national motives to the whole body of Abolitionists in the States for such a course. For I believe many of them had a fond though vain hope of seeing a day when the coloured race in the United States would be admitted to equal rights with the whites; but I believe that national prejudice may be attributed to a very large portion of them. It is a part of the principles ingrafted in their national compact, and has been carried out to the present time, without abatement, that the African race should never ascend to an equality with the whites. Not content with inoculating the length and breadth of their own land with that infernal principle, they have the audacity to attempt to insert it into foreign countries. And if Canada had not been an integral part of the glorious British Empire, they would have succeeded in it to their utmost wishes. But the Lord be thanked for the existence and maintenance of such a just and powerful nation. She has triumphed, to the great annoyance of her enemies, and will continue to do so, while she pursues the just and righteous course she has hitherto pursued. "*Righteousness exalteth a nation, but sin is a reproach to any people.*"

It was to the Abolitionists that the fugitives, fresh from the hotbeds of slavery, were directed to obtain assistance and advice on their way to Canada. Notwithstanding they knew that every coloured person going to Canada, and conducting themselves right, would enjoy as perfect freedom as they themselves, yet they would strenuously persuade and insist on them to settle in the so-called *free states*. They could not but have foreseen the evil that has come upon the fugitives in the States from the influence that slavery had over the entire Union, of which they were not ignorant. I saw it, and warned my brethren in the States of its approach. Besides, the dexterity of the slave-holders, and their northern vassals, in bringing Texas into the Union a Slave State, and the frequent attempts on the part of the United States government to negotiate with Great Britain for the delivery of fugitive slaves, who should take refuge in British territory, was, I think, sufficient to convince the most superficial observer of events, that the slave power would finally triumph through the whole Union.

Now then, in view of these remarks I beg leave to adhere to my opinion, that a large portion of the Abolitionists of the United States, who, with these evidences before them, must have been actuated by national prejudices in persuading the fugitives to stop in the States. I was informed by parties who came to this city last winter, that after the passage of the fugitive bill, the coloured people of a town in which they lived were making ready to leave in a body for Canada, but the white citizens called meetings and vehemently insisted on them not to leave, that they would protect them at all hazards. Consequently many were foolishly induced to remain. But as soon as the winter set in, and travelling became difficult, it was whispered about the town among the whites that the negroes, in that place, were to be carried back to slavery; and they were coolly told by those who had induced them to stop, that they could do nothing for them.

The United States is the most hypocritical, guileful, and arrogant nation on the face of the earth. It is far preferable for coloured people to be subjects of any other nation on earth than that. Its people rend earth and air with their protestations of freedom! They taunt other nations with tyranny! They hold large mass meetings and make declamatory speeches against other nations, and openly collect funds to assist the subjects of other nations to rebel against their governments. They send out emissaries among the people of other nations to emit their poisonous principles.

They compass sea and land to make proselytes; and when made, they are worse if possible than they are themselves. For I declare from my own knowledge that foreigners who become slave-holders in the States are more cruel than the natives. Out of many, I will mention a case or two in point. I knew an Irishman, while I lived in Washington, who was superintendent of the government grounds, attached to the President's house, and the Capitol, who had several slaves, among whom was a young man whom he struck on the head with a bar of iron, which soon caused his death. He was suspected of it, but there was no direct evidence at the time. There was a young miss, however, either coming from or going to school, who saw it through a board fence, but said nothing about it at the time; but she frequently related the circumstance after she grew to be a woman, and among others she told it to Mr. Torry. One of the Irishman's slaves I had the pleasure to deprive him of, and she is now in this city.

Again, I knew a Scotchman, Turnbull was his name. He was so severe to his slaves that they used to run off into the bush. One of them fled to the bush in winter, and after being there a few days became so pinched with cold and hunger, that he determined to return to his master; but through fear, he gave himself up to one Eatten, a slave-catcher, and requested him to intercede for him. Eatten went with him, and found his master's son at home. The old man not being at home, the son was for being down on him at once, but Eatten prevented him. When the master came, the first sight he had of the poor fellow he up with a billet of wood and let him have it across the shoulder blade. Afterwards his mistress ordered him into her room, with some wood, and noticing his walk, she ordered him to take off his shoes and stockings to see what was the matter with his feet, in doing which his feet being so frosted the skin came off with the stockings. This, together with the shoulder blade being broken from the stroke his master gave him, terminated in his death.

The people of the United States arrogate to themselves the right to meddle with the affairs of others. But oh! if the Hon. George Thompson, or some other philanthropist crosses the Atlantic to America, and raises his voice against the most inhuman system that ever blackened the pages of history, immediately there is a hue and cry among them, "hands off," "no foreign interference." Now then I will give my opinion of the United States, caring not who may demur thereto, nor what may be said thereof.

In the first place, I premise that the people of the United States will never voluntarily grant the African race among them freedom. Secondly, I liken them to the Egyptians on the one hand, and to the Jewish nation on the other. First then, God will not scourge or punish nations no more than he will individuals before he gives them due and faithful warning of the consequences of their repeated and manifold sins, and gives them a space for repentance, that they may turn from the error of their ways, cease to do evil, and learn to do well. On the other hand, if they refuse to repent in the day of grace that is given them to follow after righteousness (Jeremiah 8:20), then does he leave them in their folly to work out their own destruction. "I also will choose their delusions, and will bring their fears upon them; because when I called, none did answer; when I spake, they did not hear: but they did evil before mine eyes, and chose that in which I delighted not." (Isaiah 66:4) They fear their slaves will learn wisdom, and break off their fetters and assert their freedom. So they will. Neither will God be intreated in their behalf when they are thus left to themselves. See Jeremiah 7:15; also chapters 11:15, and 14:11. For then they have sinned unto death. See the first epistle of John 5:16.

Secondly, I shall draw an analogy between the United States and Egypt. "And the Lord said, I have surely seen the affliction of my people which are in Egypt, and have heard their cry by reason of their taskmasters; for I know their sorrows; and I am come down to deliver them out of the hand of the Egyptians;" (Exodus 3:7-8) And in the tenth verse, he says to Moses, "Come now therefore, and I will send thee unto Pharaoh, that thou mayest bring forth my people the children of Israel out of Egypt." In the nineteenth and twentieth verses of the same chapter he tells Moses as follows, "And I am sure that the King of Egypt will not let you go, no, not by a mighty hand. And I will stretch out my hand, and smite Egypt with all my wonders which I will do in the midst thereof; and then he will let you go." Hence their die was cast, and their destiny sealed: they had sinned out their day of grace (as I believe the United States has). Therefore God had determined to punish them with an overthrow while delivering his people out of their grasp. Hence Moses and Aaron bore their mission to Pharaoh. That heathen King supposed that there was no higher power than that which his fathers, he, and his advisers had established in Egypt. "And Pharaoh said, Who is the Lord that I should obey his voice to let Israel go? I know not the Lord, neither will I let Israel go." (Exodus 5:2) So that instead of relaxation, they caused an increase of pressure on the people.

In like manner the rulers of the United States are acting. When the wise men, the sorcerers, the magicians, and astrologers of the United States were assembled at Washington, casting their rods in opposition to the servants of God, to see how they could further oppress the children of Ham, by opening a way through Mason's and Dixon's sea, that they might recapture those that had crossed, they attempted to expel from their hall a servant of God, the Hon. Mr. Seward, for telling them that there was a higher power than their constitution. But many of the children of Ham, like the children of Reuben, Gad, and Manasseh, who took their inheritance beyond Jordan (Joshua 13:8), have taken inheritance beyond Lake Ontario. The result is their oppressors are in hot pursuit to carry them back into bondage; but I believe that it will end in their overthrow, as it did the Egyptians at the Red Sea. The Jews became proud, and puffed up, because God had chosen them for his peculiar people. Their great prosperity, as a nation, made them blind to their wickedness, and the sacred oracles, which God committed to them for the rule of their practice, they perverted to justify themselves in it. God, who, as before stated, will not punish his creatures before giving them due warning, and a further space for repentance, sent to them prophets, and teachers, of their own brethren; men of the greatest abilities; they had clear conceptions of the will of God concerning them, and they taught and warned their brethren against their unbounded wickedness, faithfully, that they should turn from their evil doing; but they revolted more and more (Isaiah 1:5) and killed the prophets and stoned them which were sent unto them and their land was left unto them desolate (Matthew 23:37-38). So God blotted them out from among the nations of the earth.

Are not the United States in a similar position to that of the Egyptian and Jewish nations? They have been warned of their wickedness: their own brethren, of great abilities and virtues, have written and spoken to them against it, and warned them against the dreadful consequences that will inevitably overtake them if they continue to oppress the African race, and shed the blood of the Indians. But what has been their conduct, has it not been like that of the Jews? They have imprisoned all they could lay hands on, and otherwise persecuted them, even unto death. I believe the long suspended blow against that republic and the final emancipation of their victims are close at hand, and will be attended with a terrible and bloody breaking up of their present system. No one knows nor can know the cruelties practised upon the slaves in the United States but those who commit them, and the slaves themselves. The slave-holders are very careful to keep the world in ignorance of their brutalities to their slaves. Hence travellers going among them, being loaded with their hospitality, leave with an impression that slavery is not so bad as people say it is, whereas they have not been permitted to look behind the scenes. Besides, the slave-holders make use of many arts to make strangers believe they are very good to their slaves; even to the mean practice (some of them) of taking a piece of meat skin, daily, and making their slaves grease the outside of their lips, and then take the same piece of skin and throw it up in the air to see which would be smartest in getting it to eat. This is done to have people believe they feed them well.

It can be nothing but the servile principle, for which the coloured people of the United States are so proverbial, that induces them to remain there, under its unequal laws. No matter how mean nor how bad the character (in the Slave States) of a white person, his or her oath goes before that of a coloured person, no matter how respectable, nor how much he may have at stake. In a word, the oath of a coloured person is not allowed against a white person in any matter whatever. On the other hand, it only requires the oath of the meanest white person in that country, unsupported with any other evidence, to dispossess the most respectable coloured person of all he or she has. It is true, the coloured people have as good a right to live in the United States, and enjoy the fat of the land, as their oppressors, but "*might overcomes right*" *where tyrants rule.* Did not our fathers fight side by side with their fathers, against the sires of the best friends they now have, to win that independence they now so much boast of? Yes they did! And the only reward they received is a refusal on their part to permit them to enjoy a share of the freedom they had so nobly helped them to gain, and to oppress their children down to the last turn of the screw. Yes, they even refused to grant a pension to the few shattered remains of those coloured regiments that fought so bravely in their continental army, and who received great credit from their officers.

I knew one, by name John Carey. This man lived until he was one hundred and fourteen years of age, and in the hundred and thirteenth year of his life the magnanimous Congress of the United States gave him a pension, which amounted to enough at the end of his life to bury him. The Reverend Obadiah Brown, a distinguished Baptist Minister, stated while addressing a congregation at his funeral, that he was in the whole of the seven years war during the revolution; sometimes fighting in the ranks, and at other times waiting on the person of General Washington. The coloured people have helped to clear their lands; worked their cotton, rice, sugar, and tobacco plantations. They have helped to build their cities, but it is not convenient for the coloured people to stay among them, because they oppress them; and it is a disgrace for them to stay when they can get away. Thank the Lord there is a land on the continent of America that they can get to, and have the best national freedom in the world, let who will say otherwise; where they may, through industry, prosper and multiply, until they become a terror to their enemies on the other side; and bid defiance to that much-desired project (by some)— annexation. For no coloured person who has once tasted British freedom in truth and knows how to appreciate it, will tamely submit to have it transferred to his enemies, to have it dealt with according to their rule, for the gratification of a yankee-loving faction, when they know so well what that rule is. They will present so formidable a front against annexation, that it can only be swept away with their lives.

They abolished the external or African slave trade in 1808, the effect of which gave an impetus to the infamous traffic of slave-breeding and -trading among themselves; and perhaps it was one of the main objects they had in view, the protection of their slave-breeders and -traders. I find, in a Liberty Party work, the following account of the export of slaves from 1830 to 1840, from seven of the old Slave States, viz. Maryland, Virginia, North Carolina, South Carolina, Georgia, Kentucky, and Tennessee, to the new Slave States, 431,278. According to Mr. Clay's average estimate, $400 for each slave, the whole amount of value for that number is put down at $172,511,200. Who can calculate the amount of suffering occasioned by the sudden snapping of conjugal and parental ties, among those poor creatures, by an unrighteous law, of that republic, for the gratification of about 248,711 slave-holders, in a nation of about 30,000,000? Nothing but the day of judgement can bring it to light, when all secrets will be revealed with regard to the foregoing facts. It is hard to believe them sincere. Although they have abolished the external slave trade, they have continued to nurture and foster an internal one. Besides, the supineness of the United States Naval Officers in suppressing the African slave trade is a manifest evidence that both they, and their government, connive at it.

How many captures of slavers did they make between 1808 (that being the time they abolished the African slave trade) and 1840? Not one I believe! Yet, between those periods I find it calculated in the above mentioned work, that the number of 3,880,000 were carried to Brazil, Cuba, Puerto Rico, French Colonies, and the United States. Now can anyone believe that had not the American officers and their government connived at it they could have failed to make some captures in that time? I said to an American gentleman in 1840, that while the British officers were covering themselves with immortal fame in suppressing the African slave trade, the American officers were covering themselves with immortal infamy, by doing nothing towards it. I asked him if he could tell me of a single capture of a slaver made by American officers. But he did not nor could tell me *of one!* No wonder. They connived at it while some of their most distinguished men were only a few years ago engaged in the traffic; perhaps some are now.

I remember a few years since, in a debate in the United States Senate, that a Southern Senator by way of retort upon Senator Knight, of Rhode Island, stated the following circumstance in which his (Senator Knight's) colleague had been engaged. He was a great slave-holder, and slave-trader, and on one occasion he had a cargo of slaves, and the smallpox got among them, and in order to get rid of those among his cargo infected with it, he caused a plank to be laid across the gunwale of the vessel, near a balance, and then made the poor creatures walk out on it, and so they were cast into the sea. If any of the readers of this narrative remember a few years ago that a certain dignitary died in Providence, Rhode Island, whose coffin was ornamented with solid silver, and the vault was broken into and his coffin robbed of its ornaments, that was the man who committed that infamous act. A retribution for the way he got it. He robbed the poor Africans, and his tomb was robbed in turn, and it is well for him if he be suffering no other punishment for it.

One thing more I should have noticed in another connection. The coloured seamen of the United States petitioned Congress to protect them from imprisonment when they sailed to American and Spanish slave ports, but Congress refused to receive their petition. Not long after the Americans expected to have gone to war with Britain, the coloured seamen being wide awake, knowing that they would want their services in their Navy, as they had before, held a meeting in New York City, and there passed resolutions recommending all coloured men not to enter the United States' service, in case of war. Some of them stated that fifteen hundred coloured seamen lay in a British prison at one time, taken prisoners while fighting in the American service. But the mist of American generosity has been dispelled from the eyes of the coloured people. The time was that the coloured people of the United States were easily deceived. In the last war with England, they had a good pretext to induce the coloured people to join their ranks, and not go over to the English, because they held slaves at that time also. They would tell their slaves that the English wanted them to make sale of in the West Indies, for prize money. This deterred many. But some, having very cruel masters, ventured, believing no doubt that their condition could be made no worse, while there was a chance for it to be made better. And it was made better, as many of their descendants in Nova Scotia can testify. No doubt there would be some servile coloured men fighting in the ranks of the American army in case of war, as there was in the Mexican war: base fools! Fighting for territory to perpetuate the slavery of their brethren. If I were in an army opposed to an American army, I could have more sympathy for the men of any other nation found in their ranks, than for those of my own colour, or race. And if such were the case, they might look for but little mercy from me, for I look upon such as a curse to our race, wherever found, and the sooner they are from among us the better.

The coloured men of the present generation are of no service to themselves, in the general, nor will they be to their posterity; and if their example be followed by their descendants, it will be a withering curse to them. They have neither energy nor courage. They are never found in unfrequented paths of enterprise. They are content to follow in the wake of the white man, and that very far behind; and to be hewers of wood and drawers of water, and hardly those. If the example of a few of my coloured brethren, whom I visited at the Queen's Bush, in 1843, was more generally followed by my coloured brethren in America, they would soon be worth something. Those men had settled there with no means whatever. They had to go fifteen miles out into the settlements, and there work for the farmers a fortnight, to get provision sufficient to enable them to work one week in clearing their own land. And while I was there, they were making their three meals a day on potatoes and salt. This was their language to me, "Friend Smallwood, you see how we have to live here, but we are willing to bear it, until we can get a foothold." I visited them again about three years after, the same men. Some had four, some five, and some six hundred bushels of wheat in their barns, with a good portion of stock, and everything else necessary for comfort around them. Thus, instead of having to go into the settlements to work for provision, they could hire men to work for them, and send their teams out with wheat, which brought them cash.

But how few of my brethren do I find possessed of a resolution like those men. Instead of that, they are flying from city to city, seeking employment at the hotels, and steamboats; as waiters, cooks, and barbers. Their highest ambition is to be a good waiter, or barber, and then they are made. Even many of those who have obtained mechanical trades have abandoned them, to follow those low callings; their trades being too high a degree for their low minds. Well might Walker say in his *Appeal*, in reference to our race in the United States, that they "are the most degraded, wretched, and abject set of beings that ever lived since the world began, and I pray God, that none like us ever may live again until time shall be no more." I sanction his prayer, and say, amen, let it be so.

In closing this narrative, I very much regret that I have not the manuscripts of the various articles which appeared in the Albany *Patriot*, over the signature of Samuel Weller, in 1842 and 1843, to append to this narrative, in addition to the letter appended. Being so beset by the slave-hunters before I left Washington, I was compelled to destroy them, for fear of detection.

---

*I left Mr. Torry in Baltimore, Maryland, in December, 1843. He was, if my memory be not at fault, arrested in July, 1844, in Baltimore, on a demand of the Governor of Virginia upon the Governor of Maryland, to be delivered over to the authorities of the former, under a charge of bringing out of Virginia two children to their mother, into a land of freedom. Pending his examination under that charge, there was another preferred against him, of having accomplished the escape of a woman with her two children out of Baltimore, into a land of freedom. This latter charge having been established to the satisfaction of the slave-holders, it took the precedence of the first; so that the Virginia claim fell until the Maryland law was satisfied, by his incarceration for six years in the Maryland State Prison. Had not death terminated his earthly career before his term of imprisonment expired, in all probability he would have been handed over to the tender mercies of Virginia, to satisfy her slave laws.

# *Appendix*

There is one fact which I must notice, which I would not have done but under existing circumstances. In 1847, Joseph Carter came to me while at a convention in Drummondville, Canada West, with a due bill in his possession for a certain amount of money, which had been given to him in Scotland, for the purpose, as he informed me, of trying to get one or two sisters, with their children, out of slavery. He had left the money in the hands of a gentleman in Scotland, and as soon as he could get someone to consent to try and get them for him, he was to send the due bill for the money. He therefore requested me to undertake it for him. I refused, because I had had enough of getting slaves off, at the risk of my own freedom, with but little thanks, and a plenty of abuse. However, I referred him to Elder E.B. Dunlop, who was then acting as agent for the Anti-Slavery Societies of Canada West. But he did not undertake it.

About one year after Carter applied to me again, and earnestly urged me to undertake the task for him. Finally I consented, and advised him to get Mr. Peter Brown to send the due bill for the money, which he did, and he requested Mr. Brown to hand over the money to me when it should come to hand, because he was living in the States. When the money came, I received $140 (leaving a balance of $60 in Mr. Brown's hands) and paid it to Carter, and took his receipt for it, which I now have in my possession. We then went to Cincinnati (that being at the line dividing Kentucky and Ohio, for they were in Kentucky when Carter left that State) to consult some of the most active men of the underground railroad, as to the best mode of operation, in order to succeed in getting them. Every plan suggested on our part was considered impracticable, owing to the fact that a white friend of those whom we consulted, had, not long before that, left Cincinnati with the intention to bring one hundred slaves out of Kentucky, and who was betrayed with that number near the line, or Ohio River, by two of the number, who gave him the slip, and informed against him, and he was taken with the slaves. That circumstance deprived us of his assistance, while it also created so great an excitement and vigilance on the Kentucky side of the Ohio river, that after remaining eleven days trying to see what could be done, we were advised to return and wait for a more favourable time. I have letters from Cincinnati, now in my possession, in confirmation of the above statements.

## *Demoralizing Influence of Slavery*

The demoralizing influence of slavery is seen among the whites and the blacks in the Slave States. For instance, behold the frequent resort that is had to pistols, swords, and bowie knives, among the Southerners; and the cold-blooded murders in affairs of (what they call) honour. They have not yet wiped away the stain of the blood of the venerable Professor Davis, who was murdered a few years since by one of his students, for doing his duty towards him, for his good, by bringing him to just punishment. No! he was admitted to bail in the sum of $25,000, and sent out of the way until the bail was forfeited and paid by his wealthy parents. And so the matter ended, and a valuable life sold for $25,000, to gratify the blood-thirsty spirit of slavery.

With regard to the coloured people of the Slave States, the demoralizing influence of slavery is more particularly seen among the females, although it unavoidably extends to the males. For instance, female chastity among them is not protected by law, nor respected by the whites. Their virtue is tampered with, trampled on, violated, and is entirely at the mercy and will of any and every debauchee who chooses to arm himself with the advantages he has over the poor coloured female; and they are neither few nor far between. Hence, there is no stimulation to virtue among the females; and the males, knowing that, are equally regardless of that great principle. For if one should chance to get a virtuous companion, her fidelity to him is almost sure to be destroyed by some white man. It matters not whether they be free or bond, the result is the same. The easy and luxurious life of the Southerners, by means of slave labour, disposes them to this species of vice. For the oppression of the African race in the South, the North need not think to escape the just punishment due to it. For the Northerners are the slave-holders, while the Southerners are the drivers, and they divide the spoil of their labour between them.

## *The Conduct of the Coloured People in Canada, Impolitic*

The policy of the coloured people in separating themselves from the white religious connections in Canada, of whose persuasions they are, into distinct little bodies, is a bar to their moral and religious elevation, as well as to their domestic elevation. I am free to admit that in the United States, where the laws make a distinction between the rights of the white and the coloured people, there were strong grounds for a separation, for the policy of the churches there is the same as that of the state: they deprive their coloured members of the rights enjoyed by their white members. That, unfortunately, has engendered a prejudice in the minds of many of the coloured people against being in connection with the white people. But I warn my coloured brethren who are flying from their oppressors to these shores of freedom for all, and who are not only welcomed with outstretched arms by our white brethren, who extend the hand of relief to their necessities, not to bring that spirit to this country. We want none of it here.

The British people are not slave-holders! The British laws make no distinction between man and man on account of colour! It would be absurd, in the highest degree, for my strange brethren, who have sought freedom in this country, to seek to introduce and keep up a diabolical system that was forced upon them in a slave-holding country. It is our business to identify our interest with that of our white fellow citizens, and to form the most intimate relations with them of which our circumstances in life will admit. They have, under God, all the wealth, influence, and power. How dare we then, poor refugees, to say, as I understand some have said, that, "they want nothing to do with the white people." The very people to whom they fly for freedom. We have neither learning, wealth, nor influence at the present. It is to them, under God, that we owe our present freedom. With what grace, then, can we complain of prejudice against us, while we ourselves are the promoters thereof? There are too many among us who desire the chief seats in the synagogues, whose acquirements and talents are not sufficient to entitle us to them. They obtrude their ignorance upon the ignorance of their brethren, and thus the blind lead the blind.

The following letter is one of a number of letters written by me, between eight and nine years ago, from Washington, and published in the Albany *Weekly Patriot*, about that time, portraying the doings of the slave-holders. The assumed name, Samuel Weller, Jr., was made use of to avoid detection, because a number of copies of every issue of that paper containing those letters were sent to each person of whom they treated. Those letters were a great annoyance to the slave-holders in that section, and they would have been very glad to have got the writer.

— *T.S.*

## *Washington Correspondence*

*Freemen Made Slaves!— Kidnapping in Washington!— More of the Auxilliary Guard!*

For the *Albany Weekly Patriot*

Washington, D.C.
June 6, 1843

*Mr. Editor,* I have some things of much interest to communicate, that I write again sooner than anticipated.

Twelve years ago a Mrs. Hardy of Maryland died, leaving all her slaves, by her will, to her brother, Basil Hatten, with a provision that they, *with their increase*, should be free at his death. There was a farther provision that, if any were not of age, they should be put to trades— the males till they were twenty-one, the females till they were eighteen.

Hatten died just about twelve years after his sister. The people being now free, many of them removed to this city.

Mr. Robert Hunter, the heir-at-law, claims as his slaves all the children who were born between Mrs. Hardy's death, and the death of her brother, notwithstanding the clause in the will to free the "increase." He claims that they do not come under the provisions of the will, and that the "increase" refers to the children already born, at the time Mrs. Hardy died.

Some of them were pretty well advanced, though not of age. But he made no provision for them, nor attempted in any way to control them, with but one exception. He *fooled* one to remain with him on his plantation. The rest he could not deceive; so he cared nothing for them.

In order to carry out his designs against the children, he employed certain noted slave-hunters in Maryland to come to this city and kidnap them, which they did; six in number. They came on the *Sabbath Day*, just about church time, that there might not be an uproar. They stole them, and carried them into Maryland. The case is now in law. The result is very uncertain.

This is not the only instance of kidnapping in Washington. I know a coloured man named Henry Chubb, who sometimes worked about the dock, loading and unloading vessels. He, with two of his sons, had been unloading a vessel, and after discharging her, he went ashore, leaving his sons to clear out the hold of the vessel. In the meantime the captain set sail and carried the two sons into slavery, to the unspeakable grief of their parents, who were both *free born!*

Similar acts have often been done, and are still doing, in this metropolis of *free* and *Christian* America; whose free institutions (!!) are so much admired; and who keep God's children in abject slavery, and utter ignorance, with as much boldness as if an express command from God sanctioned the atrocity! Do Americans think that the rest of the world has not sense enough to see and despise their hypocrisy?

I come now to notice the death of a Christian and patriot, in the person of John Carey. He died on the 2d ultimo, about nine o'clock p.m. No person, I presume, in this city, has enjoyed a greater degree of the confidence of the public on account of his *truly* Christian example. He was a member of the First Baptist Church. The body was brought into the meeting house on the Sabbath afternoon, attended by several clergymen. The Pastor, Reverend Obadiah Brown, delivered an excellent discourse. He stated that Carey was born in Westmoreland County, Virginia, in 1729, as he had learned from documents that he had recently seen. This made him one hundred and fourteen years old next August. General Washington, who knew how to appreciate worth in a black, as well as in a white man, chose him for his body servant. He was with him in the old French war, at Braddock's defeat, and throughout the revolution. He was often in the ranks, helping to fight the battles of his country. At the close of the war, General Washington gave him one of his regimental coats, which he always wore, especially on public occasions.

And what reward did the *grateful Republic* give him for his services? Why, a few months before his death, by the exertions of Hon. George N. Briggs, of Pittsfield, Massachusetts, Congress was induced to pass a bill giving him a pension, for the rest of his life. He received about enough to bury him decently! Most grateful country! Most magnanimous Congress!

I wish to bestow a passing notice on the Auxilliary Guard. Don't let the people forget these scoundrels! They have established a *new branch of business*, which is, to station themselves in the streets, near the meeting houses of the coloured people, and watch if any are later than ten o'clock returning home, to compel them to pay fines if they are free, or else send them to the workhouse. If they are slaves their masters must pay, or they are whipped, for the *crime of attending on the public worship of God*, a few moments later than ten o'clock! John Little and William Cox are very active in this business. Little is too lazy to support his family in any other way; and he is as famous for administering *discipline* to his wife! as he is for negro hunting! How long will the people of the North agree to support these scoundrels?

You remember my telling you, that in the recess of Congress, the coloured people suffer much more than when Congress is here. It has been peculiarly so, since the last session. God help the poor defenceless ones!

*Yours for liberty,*
*Samuel Weller, Jr.*

# EXPLANATORY NOTES

Important quotations, people, places and events mentioned by Smallwood, and which might not be obviously known today, have been briefly explained. These notes are linked to the text by page and line number. The following abbreviations are used throughout the notes: DAH (*Dictionary of American History*), DAS (*Dictionary of Afro-American Slavery*), DAF (*Dictionary of American Foreign Affairs*), DNB (*Dictionary of National Biography*), and EACH (*Encyclopaedia of African-American Culture and History*).

*23.8-12 Semiramis- Nimrod- Sardinapolis*

Semiramis (c. 800 B.C.) was Queen and Regent of Assyria. In *Who's Who in the Ancient Near East*, Gwendolyn Leick notes that according "to a recently discovered stele [stone monument] she accompanied the king on a military campaign, an event otherwise unheard of in Assyrian history... She became the subject of later legendary tales, and is mentioned by Herodotus as the builder of embankments in Babylon."(143) Nimrod is the legendary Assyrian hunter and founder of cities who is described in the Old Testament Book of Genesis, 10:8-12. Sardanapalus is identified in the *Encyclopaedia of the Roman Empire* as "the last ruler of the Assyrian Empire."(374)

*23.20 the voice of Stentor*

Stentor is a figure from Greek mythology. He appears in Homer's *Iliad:* "great-hearted Stentor of the brazen voice, who could shout as loud as fifty other men."(5.785-6) According to the *Cassell Dictionary of Classical Mythology*, Stentor was "killed for his presumption in claiming that he could shout as mightily as Hermes, the herald of the gods. His name has survived in 'stentorian,' meaning 'uncommonly loud.'"(361)

*23.24 Jehovah thundering out of Zion*

John Milton, the English poet, lived between 1608 and 1675. He published *Paradise Lost: A Poem Written in Ten Books* in London in 1667. Smallwood's quotation is from Book I, lines 386-387. As Scott Elledge comments, in this passage Milton "identifies certain fallen angels as spirits who later became the false gods of Isarael's neighbouring nations."(19n) Smallwood's quotation is taken from the following context:

The chief were those who from the pit of hell
Roaming to seek their prey on earth, durst fix
Their seats long after next the seat of God,
Their altars by his altar, gods adored
Among the nations round, and durst abide
Jehovah thund'ring out of Zion, throned
Between the Cherubim...

*23.28 cities of the Plains*
Smallwood draws a comparison between the United States and the biblical cities of the Plain, the best known of which are Sodom and Gomorrah. Smallwood quotes from the Old Testament Book of Genesis, 13:12: "Abram settled in the land of Canaan, while Lot settled among the cities of the Plain... Now the people of Sodom were wicked, great sinners against the Lord."

*23.29 "all men are born equal..."*
I have been unable to find a source corroborating this as a quotation of Napoleon Bonaparte.

*24.3 "In the sight of our law..."*
Smallwood quotes from Daniel Webster's famous "Plymouth Oration," delivered on December 22, 1820, at Plymouth, Massachusetts, in commemoration of the two-hundredth anniversary of the landing of the Pilgrims. Webster prefaces the extract Smallwood quotes in the following way: "The true principle of a free and popular government would seem to be, so to construct it as to give to all, or at least to a very great majority, an interest in its preservation... I deem it my duty on this occasion to suggest, that the land is not wholly free from the contamination of a traffic, at which every feeling

of humanity must for ever revolt— I mean the African slave trade."(Lewis, 85)

*24.8 "darkness is over the face of the earth"*
Here Smallwood appears to be misquoting the Old Testament Book of Genesis 1:1-2, which reads, "darkness was upon the face of the deep."

*24.9 Nature's sweet restorer, balmy sleep*
Edward Young, the English poet, lived between 1683 and 1765. He published his immensely popular and immensely long nine-book poem, *Night Thoughts*, beginning in 1742. Smallwood quotes from line 1 of "Night the First":

Tir'd nature's sweet Restorer, balmy *Sleep*!
He, like the World, his ready visit pays,
Where Fortune smiles; the wretched he forsakes;
Swift on his downy pinion flies from woe,
And lights on Lids unsully'd with a Tear.

*24.11 The parenthesis of human woe*
I have been unable to find this phrase in the works of Samuel Johnson.

*24.13 Sleep, great nature's second course*
I have been unable to find this phrase in the works of Edward Young.

*24.19 "Talk not to me of rights..."*
Henry Lord Brougham, English politician, lived between 1778 and 1868. He delivered his famous "Speech on Negro Slavery" in the British House of Commons on July 13, 1830. Smallwood may have read Brougham's speech in the collected *Speeches of Henry Lord Brougham* published in Philadelphia in 1841. Near the end of this version of the speech, Brougham says, "Tell me not of rights— talk not of the property of the planter in his slaves. I deny the right— I acknowledge not the property. The principles, the feelings of our

common nature, rise in rebellion against it... In vain you tell me of laws that sanction such a claim! There is a law above all the enactments of human codes..."(438)

*25.1 "the flood of British Freedom..."*

William Wordsworth, the English poet, lived between 1770 and 1850. He wrote the series of poems known variously as the "Sonnets Dedicated to Liberty" or "Poems Dedicated to Independence and Liberty" between 1802 and 1803, although some were not published until much later. Smallwood quotes from Sonnet XVI, part of a four-sonnet sequence entitled "London, 1802":

It is not to be thought of that the Flood
Of British freedom, which to the open sea
Of the world's praise, from dark antiquity
Hath flowed, "with pomp of waters, unwithstood,"
Roused though it be full often to a mood
Which spurns the check of salutary bonds,
That this most famous Stream in bogs and sands
Should perish...

As John Williams argues, the sonnets embody a "position critical of [Wordsworth's] country's political establishment."(141)

*25.6 "I speak in the spirit of British law..."*

I have been unable to find these remarks among the collected speeches of John Philpot Curran.

*25.18 I would not have a slave to till my ground*

William Cowper, the English poet, lived between 1731 and 1800. He was also an unsuccessful lawyer and later a curate at Olney in Buckinghamshire. Cowper's DNB entry calls the "pathos of some of the minor poems...

unsurpassed."(1326) Smallwood quotes from Book II, lines 29-30, of Cowper's long poem "The Task," written in 1785:

Thus man devotes his brother, and destroys;
And worse than all, and most to be deplored
As human nature's broadest, foulest blot,
Chains him, and tasks him, and exacts his sweat
With stripes, that mercy with a bleeding heart
Weeps when she sees inflicted on a beast.
Then what is man? And what man seeing this,
And having human feelings, does not blush
And hang his head, to think himself a man?
I would not have a slave to till my ground,
To carry me, to fan me while I sleep,
And tremble when I wake, for all the wealth
That sinews bought and sold have ever earn'd.

*26.6 By seraphs writ with beams of heavenly light*
Quotation from line 10 of William Cowper's poem "To Mary Unwin":

There is a Book
By seraphs writ with beams of heavenly light,
On which the eyes of God not rarely look,

A chronicle of actions just and bright—
There all thy deeds, my faithful Mary, shine;
And since thou own'st that praise, I spare thee mine.

*26.10 UNITED STATES! Your banner wears two emblems—*
Thomas Campbell, the Scottish poet, lived between 1777 and 1844. He wrote the poem entitled "Epigram to the United States of North America," in 1838. Smallwood reproduces the full text of the poem in his Preface to the *Narrative*.

*26.21 Of that green land, cradled in the roar*

Percy Bysshe Shelley, the English poet, lived between 1792 and 1822. The poem Smallwood quotes, "The Revolt of Islam," has a complicated textual history. Shelley originally published it in 1817 under the title "Laon and Cyntha," but the subject matter, which included revolution and incest, caused the poem to be censored. Shelley decided to republish the poem the following year under a new title. Smallwood was probably attracted to Shelley's stated aims in his Preface to "The Revolt of Islam." "It is an experiment," Shelley writes, "on the temper of the public mind, as to how far a thought for a happier condition of moral and political society survives... the tempests which have shaken the age in which we live."(85) Smallwood's quotation is taken from the following context in Canto V, Verse LI:

Victory! Victory! Earth's remotest shore,
Regions which groan beneath the Antarctic stars,
The green lands cradled in the roar
Of western waves and wilderness
Peopled and vast, which skirt the oceans
Where morning dyes her golden tresses,
Shall soon partake our high emotions:
Kings shall turn pale! Almighty Fear...
Shall fade like shadow from his thousand fanes,
While truth with Joy enthroned o'er his lost empire reigns!

*26.25 That a land of slaves shall ne'er be mine*

George Gordon, Lord Byron, the English poet, lived between 1788 and 1824. Smallwood quotes from Canto III, Verse 16 of one of Byron's best-known poems, *Don Juan*, the third to fifth cantos of which were published in 1821:

Place me on Sunium's marbled steep,
Where nothing, save the waves and I,
May hear our mutual murmurs sweep;
There, swan-like, let me sing and die;

A land of slaves shall ne'er be mine—
Dash down your cup of Sensian wine!

*27.3 A footstep was heard in the rustling brake*
I have been unable to find this phrase in the works of Henry Wadsworth Longfellow.

*27.11 Wha sae base as be a slave*
Robert Burns, the Scottish poet, lived between 1759 and 1796. The historical poem "Robert Bruce's March to Bannockburn" was written in 1793. Smallwood quotes from the third stanza:

Scots, wha hae wi' Wallace bled,
Scots, whan Bruce has aften led,
Welcome to your gory bed—
Or to victorie.—

Now's the day, and now's the hour;
See the front o' battle lour;
See approach proud EDWARD's power,
Chains and Slaverie.—

Wha will be a traitor-knave?
Wha can fill a coward's grave?
Wha sae base as be a slave?
—Let him turn and flie...—

*27.23 Slander lives upon succession*
William Shakespeare, the English actor, playwright, and poet, lived between 1564 and 1616. *The Comedy of Errors* was first performed in 1594, and Smallwood quotes from Act 3, Scene 1, lines 104-105, from a speech by the character Balthazar.

*28.3 Slander/ Whose edge is sharper than the sword*

Shakespeare's *Cymbeline* was first performed around 1610. Smallwood quotes Act 3, Scene 4, lines 32-35, from a speech by the character Pisanio.

*28.7 Clarkson and Wilberforce*

The DNB summarizes Thomas Clarkson, who lived between 1760 and 1846, in the following way: "Clarkson was not the first to call the attention of the country to the criminality of slavery, but it is almost impossible to overrate the effect of his unceasing perseverance in the cause."(455) Clarkson's 1786 publication, "An Essay on the Slavery and Commerce of the Human Species, particularly the African," inaugurated a life-long career as an anti-slavery agitator. Together with William Wilberforce, who lived between 1759 and 1833, the well-known politician, philanthropist and anti-slavery proponent, they founded the Anti-Slavery Society in 1823. Wilberforce was the chief architect of the 1807 bill that abolished the slave trade, and as the DNB puts it, "Wilberforce was henceforth the object of unique respect... the authorised interpreter of the national conscience."(214)

*29.1 George Thompson*

English anti-slavery advocate and politician, Thompson lived between 1804 and 1878. His DNB entry states that he "first became widely known as an advocate of the abolition of slavery in the British colonies."(691) Thompson was in the mid-1830s so unpopular in some quarters in the United States, that he had to escape from Boston by ship in 1835. He was elected to the British parliament in 1847, and was subsequently given a public reception in the United States, attended by President Lincoln.

*29.3 His life was gentle, and the elements so mixed in him*

Shakespeare's *Julius Caesar* was first performed in 1599. Smallwood quotes Antony's famous speech near the end of the play, from Act 5, Scene 5, lines 74-76.

### *30.11 Walker's* Appeal

David Walker, who lived between 1785 and 1830, was born in Wilmington, North Carolina. His mother was a free Black and his father was a slave. The DAS says that "according to the law of his home state, [Walker] assumed the free status of his mother."(791) Settling eventually in Boston, Walker became active in Black anti-slavery circles, especially arguing against colonization. In 1829, Walker published *David Walker's Appeal, in Four Articles; Together with a Preamble to the Coloured Citizens of the World, But in Particular, and Very Expressly to Those of the United States of America.* In his DAS entry on Walker, Jason Silverman argues that Walker's *Appeal* both "implored all black people to rise in violent insurrection," but also "profferred a gesture of Christian forgiveness, suggesting that peace and harmony would prevail should the slave-holders free their slaves voluntarily."(791) Walker's *Appeal* was banned in most Southern states, and "a price was placed upon Walker's head."(792) Walker died in suspicious circumstances outside his clothing shop in Boston.

### *30.16 Henry Highland Garnet*

Garnet, who lived between 1815 and 1882, is described in EACH as "one of the most formidable African-American leaders of the mid-nineteenth century."(1087) Born a slave, Garnet escaped to New York City with his family. After receiving an excellent education, Garnet became a minister in the Presbyterian church in 1843. His church was "an important station on the underground railroad."(1088) Increasingly radical in his politics, Garnet delivered his famous "Address to the Slaves of the United States of America" at Buffalo in 1843. Garnet's speech was interpreted as a call to slave rebellion. Garnet later became president of the African Colonisation Society which promoted emigration to Africa. As his EACH entry puts it, even though "the ACS gradually turned its missionary impulse toward meeting the relief and education needs of the freed people during and after the Civil War, Garnet never relinquished his vision of African redemption."(1088) Garnet died in Liberia, where he had served as American minister.

*34.7 "render unto Caesar the things which are Caesar's"*
Quotation from The Gospel According to Matthew, 22:21: "Render therefore unto Caesar the things which are Caesar's; and unto God the things that are God's."

*36.20 African Colonisation— that Society*
Here Smallwood refers to the American Colonization Society, founded in 1816 by a white clergyman, Robert Finley, and which operated until 1892. DAS says the Society's goal was to "settle blacks in Africa" in the hope that "colonization would eventually lead to the end of slavery."(122) Supported by some slave-owners, the Society was criticized by free Blacks and white abolitionists, as being racist. The ACS founded Liberia, the African nation, and attracted more than 10,000 colonists to that country by 1865.

*37.14 Liberia trade*
Smallwood implies he could have made a lot of money by signing up colonists for the African Colonisation Society.

*38.7 the Greeks and Poles*
Here Smallwood refers to the struggles for independence in Greece in the period 1821-1844. The Greek war for independence ended in 1821 with the establishment of a Greek state, ruled by a hereditary monarchy. In 1843, an army-led coup forced King Otto of Greece to offer his citizens a new constitution. The reference to Poland is to the November Rising of 1830-31 when Polish insurgents tried to assassinate the Russian tsar's brother (who was then acting as Viceroy of Poland). This led to the Russo-Polish War of 1831. The Poles were eventually defeated and harsh retaliatory measures were instituted by the Russian rulers.

*38.18 the fugitive bill*
In his EACH entry on Fugitive Slave Laws, Paul Finkleman argues that while the notorious 1850 Fugitive Slave Act "did much to antagonize sectional feelings,"(1072) leading to riots in Boston and Syracuse for example, it actually

didn't work very well as a tool for slave-holders to reclaim their "property." The U.S. Constitution included a provision for the return of escaped slaves to their owners, which was bolstered by the Congressional Fugitive Slave Act of 1793. Although the legality of the Act was challenged— many Northern states, for instance, "adopted 'personal-liberty laws' to protect free Blacks from kidnapping or mistaken seizure"(1071)— its constitutionality was upheld in 1842. The 1850 Act changed the situation by not allowing "alleged fugitives"(1071) to testify on their own behalf, nor to have a trial by jury. The 1850 Act also provided "for enforcement by federal commissioners to be appointed in every county in the country."(1071) These commissioners were paid five dollars if they decided the person was not a slave, and ten dollars if they determined the person was a slave.

*38.25 Daniel Webster*

Webster was an American attorney, politician, and orator, who lived between 1782 and 1852. He served as Secretary of State in two administrations, including under Abraham Lincoln. Webster's DAS entry summarizes him as a "defender of the Union and critic of slavery."(797) Smallwood's anger at Webster stems from Webster's "last concerted political effort,"(797) the Compromise of 1850. In his famous "Seventh of March Speech," Webster promoted a series of compromise measures to "quell sectional tensions"(797) and avert a civil war. These compromises included amending the Fugitive Slave Act as mentioned above. Webster's compromises were viewed as treacherous by the anti-slavery community, both Black and white.

*39.13 Rev. C.T. Torry*

Charles Turner Torry (or Torrey as his entry in *The National Cyclopaedia of American Biography* spells it) plays a large role in Smallwood's *Narrative.* According to the *Cyclopaedia,* Torrey, who lived between 1813 and 1846, was a pastor in the Congregational ministry who was also active as an anti-slavery agitator. He "went into Maryland in the service of the 'underground railroad,' which naturally brought him into collision with the local laws."(200) Torrey was arrested in 1844 after helping a number of slaves escape to the North, and sentenced to a "long term."(200) Torrey died in prison of consumption, exciting "great sympathy in the North and England, and inspired the Abolitionists with renewed zeal."(200)

*40.8 the* Patriot *of this City*
Published continuously between 1828 and 1878, the *Patriot and Farmer's Monitor* was founded in Kingston, Upper Canada, by Thomas Dalton. After December 7, 1832, the *Patriot* was published in Toronto. At the time Smallwood was reading it, the *Patriot* was, in the words of Edith G. Firth, the "paper of the English Conservatives and Church of England party."(5)

*40.27 "all men are born free and equal..."*
Quotation from the American Declaration of Independence, written in 1776 by Thomas Jefferson. "We hold these truths to be self-evident: that all men are created equal; that they are endowed by their Creator with certain unalienable rights; that among these are life, liberty, and the pursuit of happiness."

*46.12 Had I been a physiognomist*
Here Smallwood refers to the science of Physiognomy, which enjoyed immense popularity in the nineteenth century. In *Physiognomy and the European Novel,* Graeme Tytler shows how although "physiognomy has a long and illustrious history stretching back to classical antiquity"(35) it comes into its own during the career of Johann Casper Lavater (1741-1801), a Swiss pastor. Lavater's *Physiognomische Fragmente* (Leipzig, 1775-8), translated into English as *Essays on Physiognomy,* influenced numerous philosophers and writers. The basic premise of Physiognomy is that human beings can be classified and explained according to their facial characteristics. According to Lavater, Physiognomy's purpose is "to help human beings to know and love one another."(64) Smallwood's reference to Physiognomy is on one level ironic because despite Lavater's lofty moral hopes for Physiognomy, it has been used more often to argue for differences between the races and various nationalities.

*56.32 a defunct institution*

Here Smallwood refers to the Refugee Home Society, an institution which provoked a great deal of debate and anger among various factions of the Black community of Canada West. Organized in 1851, the purpose of the organization was to buy a large tract of land near Windsor on which to settle refugees from American slavery. The RHS was criticized heavily by Black Canadian leaders like Mary Shadd, who argued that the scheme was not only segregationist, but also corrupt financially. Shadd argued that land was available from the government of Canada West at better prices than from the society. The implication of Shadd's criticism is that the leaders of the RHS, among them Henry and Mary Bibb, were using the RHS to "line their own pockets," as Smallwood claims. Winks' discussion of the RHS (pp.204-208) is relatively balanced. I would like to thank Afua Cooper for providing me with new insights into the RHS.

*57.28 African Methodist Episcopal Church*

In *The Blacks in Canada,* Robin Winks writes that the African Methodist Episcopal Church "was founded in 1816 in Philadelphia by Richard Allen and fifteen other Negroes, largely in response to the growing racial exclusiveness of the parent church in the United States and also from a desire to create bishoprics which Negroes might fill."(355-6) The first AME church in Upper Canada opened in 1839. In the 1850s, the AME Church in Canada split into two factions, one which became the BME (British Methodist Episcopal) and the other which stayed AME.

*64.27 "Righteousness exalteth a nation..."*

Quotation from the Old Testament Book of Genesis, 14:34.

*65.6 Texas— a Slave State*

When Texas, which had been an independent republic since its successful revolution against Mexico in 1836, approved annexation by the United States in 1845, one of the terms set by the Texans and acceded to by the United

States was that slavery be secured as an institution in Texas. From a population of 30,000 slaves at the beginning of its statehood, the population of slaves escalated dramatically. The DAS entry on "Texas, Slavery in" says that by 1860 (fifteen years after statehood) 30.2% of the Texas population, or 182,566 persons, lived in Texas as slaves.(724-731)

*68.13 children of Ham*

The phrase refers to the biblical tradition of viewing Noah's second son, Ham, as "the ancestor of the Egyptians... as well as of peoples in Africa, Arabia, and Canaan."(Elwell,919) The phrase also refers to the "curse of Ham," which is uttered by Noah in Genesis 9:25-27: "'Cursed be Canaan; lowest of slaves shall he be to his brothers.'" This passage has resulted in an unfortunate confusion, because Noah's curse has been interpreted as being made against Ham (and hence his African descendants), instead of against Canaan, Ham's son. In the biblical story, Ham finds his father naked and drunk, and informs his brothers, who proceed to cover Noah. Noah then curses Canaan. Instead of seeing the curse as against Ham (for seeing his father's nakedness), it is now generally agreed that the curse is against Canaan, for some unspecified action.

*68.16 Hon. Mr. Seward*

Henry Seward, who lived between 1801 and 1872, was an American lawyer, state governor, and later senator. Seward was a republican presidential candidate in 1860 but lost to the less-radical Abraham Lincoln. He later became Secretary of State under Lincoln. Seward is best known for his famous remark, made during the Compromise of 1850 debates, that there is "a higher law than the constitution."(DAF, 539) Seward "opposed accommodation of the South"(539) throughout his career. As a lawyer in the 1840s, Seward had defended John Van Zandt, a white man who had given a group of Blacks he found walking along an Ohio road a ride in his wagon, and who was arrested under the Fugitive Slave Act.(DAS, 760)

*71.7 a Liberty Party work*

The DAH entry for the Liberty Party claims it was "the first anti-slavery political party... formed by opponents of William Lloyd Garrison's abolitionists in 1830."(143) In 1848, the Liberty Party merged with another anti-slavery party, the Free-Soil Party. The *Oxford Illustrated Companion to American History* describes the Free-Soil Party as developing "from opposition to the extension of slavery into any of the territories newly acquired from Mexico."(313) Although the Liberty and Free-Soil parties were never successful in electing high-ranking politicians, they did garner enough votes to affect the balance of power.

*73.21 hewers of wood and drawers of water*

Quotation from the Old Testament Book of Joshua, 9:23. The Gibeonites had tricked the Israelites into thinking they were "from a far country,"(9:6) and thus to be treated with greater leniency in Israel's expansionist settlement of Canaan. For their duplicity, they were cursed by Joshua, the Israelite military leader: "Now therefore you are cursed, and some of you shall always be slaves, hewers of wood and drawers of water for the house of my God."

*73.23 Queen's Bush*

Queen's Bush was the term used to describe that part of southwestern Canada West (present-day Ontario) roughly bounded by Lake Huron to the west, Georgian Bay to the north, and the already-settled areas like Waterloo Township to the south. It is not clear which settlement Smallwood visited in 1843, but the two most probable choices are the Wilberforce settlement just north of London (not properly part of the Queen's Bush) or else the Black settlements in present-day Oro township, in the Collingwood area. Winks, in *The Blacks in Canada*, relates this instructive anecdote: "in 1846 white residents of Brantford asked that the Negroes there— fifteen families— be sent away into Queen's Bush... Eventually a Black community grew near the Conestogo River midway between Waterloo and Guelph. Other travellers reported seeing Negro farms as far north and east as Penetanguishene, Collingwood, Owen Sound, and Barrie."(146)

*75.3 Drummondville, C.W.*

"In 1831," according to the Kiwanis Club of Stamford's history, *Niagara Falls, Canada,* "Stamford Township saw the rise of its first community. The cluster of a dozen houses around the junction of Portage Road, Lundy's Lane and Ferry Street obtained village status. The name it chose was Drummondville, in honour of Sir Gordon Drummond, leader of the British forces in the Battle of Lundy's Lane."(36) Drummondville became the town of Niagara Falls in 1881. Smallwood attended a convention of leaders of the Canadian Black community in Drummondville in 1847. See *Extracts from the Report of the Convention of the Coloured Population Held at Drummondville, August, 1847*, the next section of this book.

*75.13 Anti-Slavery Societies of Canada West*

At the time Smallwood published his *Narrative*, the Anti-Slavery Society of Canada (Smallwood incorrectly calls it "of Canada West") had just been launched. According to Winks, this "first major Canadian antislavery society was created to combat the growing evidence of organized... prejudice in Canada West."(252) Winks goes on to argue that the Society was not very effectual, often crippled by dissension amongst its members along religious lines. The Society struggled throughout its existence to move "from an emphasis on relief to a more direct expression of abolitionist sentiment."(257)

*77.5 the venerable Professor Davis*

I have been unable to find a reference either to Professor Davis or to his murder.

# APPENDIX

*The following document is one of the most important in reconstructing the life of Thomas Smallwood. Held in the Canadiana collection of the E.J. Pratt Library at Victoria University, Toronto, this slim 16-page pamphlet sheds fascinating light on the activities of the Black community of southern Ontario in the period just before the Fugitive Slave Act was passed in the United States.*

*Extracts from the*

## REPORT OF THE CONVENTION OF THE COLOURED POPULATION HELD AT DRUMMONDVILLE, AUGUST, 1847

### *The Coloured Population of Canada*

It had long been a matter of regret that there did not exist in Canada any regularly organized Society to which the individuals who escape from the slavery of the United States might look for assistance and for advice as to their future guidance. Such an Institution has become absolutely essential to the welfare of the coloured population. The friends of the long oppressed African race, residing in Canada, Great Britain, and the United States, are ever willing to assist those who escape from the land of bondage with aid to settle in their new abode, and to gain their bread by lawful industry.

But in order that this may be done with confidence, it is necessary that the management and distribution should be placed under such as would be able and faithful guardians of what was committed to them. The increasing number of the coloured population in Canada has for several years attracted the attention of the philanthropists in Great Britain and the United States, and missions have been undertaken by various individuals to these countries, to procure assistance for them.

With the money realized by one of these missions the settlement of Dawn, Sydenham, Western Canada was formed several years ago. Large sums of money and quantities of clothing have since been received from Great Britain and the United States, but it is not known how they have been disposed of. Whether there has been faithful management or not, the mass of the coloured population for whose behoof these collections were made, are generally dissatisfied, as no satisfactory account of these transactions had ever been published.

The first step taken to bring these interests into a regular business-like form was the organization of a Society some months ago entitled The British American Anti-Slavery Society. Its headquarters are at Toronto, but it is intended that it shall have branches all over the province. This society has met with the approbation of the coloured population of Toronto, and of many other friends. But something more than this was required to raise up a central power, to which the self-emancipated slave might look for protection and assistance, the distressed meet with sympathy and support in the hour of need, the interests of the coloured population be promoted, and their persons protected by prompt appeals to the justice of British law.

With a view to carry out these important objects, it was deemed advisable to hold a General Convention of the coloured population of the province. On the 7th of June last an address was extensively circulated from Toronto, and published in several newspapers, inviting a Convention to be held in Drummondville, on the 2nd day of August and subsequent days.

## THE CONVENTION

### Session I

In consequence of the said call, the Convention met at Drummondville on Monday the 2nd day of August, 1847, in the African Methodist Episcopal Chapel...

The call of the Convention having been read, on motion of Mr. Smallwood, the Delegates present were requested to present their credentials, when the following gentlemen took their seats, viz.—

Rev. Thomas Smallwood, Toronto
Mr. J.T. Henson, Dawn
...

On motion, a Committee of three was appointed by the Chairman, consisting of Messrs. Smallwood, Dunlop, and Liles, to nominate officers for the Convention...

The meeting appointed the following Committees:

On Business— Messrs. Smallwood, Ramsay, Watson, Counter, and J.T. Henson

On Finance— Messrs. Warren, Counter, and Smallwood.

Convention adjourned to 9 o'clock next morning.

### Session II
Tuesday August 3rd 9 a.m.

A letter was also read from Dawn, concerning the illegal election of one of the Delegates from that place.

Both letters were laid on for after consideration.

## Session III
### Tuesday August 3rd 3 p.m.

The Business Committee reported that they would recommend to the consideration of the Convention the latter part of the call which relates to the moral, religious, and social condition of their people, and the best means for their improvement.

Report laid on the table.

In accordance therewith, it was then

*Resolved,* That means should be taken to ascertain, as far as possible what is the condition of our people, in order that we may be enabled to devise means for their elevation...

Moved by Mr. Smallwood, and

*Resolved,* That if the monies, clothing, and other articles contributed in the United States and Great Britain had been equitably and judiciously divided, our condition would have been greater than it now is.

Laid on the table.

Moved by Mr. Smallwood, seconded by Mr. Cannon—

*Resolved,* That this Convention is satisfied that frauds have been committed upon the people of colour in Canada regarding to monies, clothing, and other articles sent from the United States and elsewhere.

Laid on the table.

Adjourned till next day.

## Session IV
### Wednesday August 4th 9 a.m.

After a long discussion in regard to the order of the day, and other minor matters, the Rev. J. Henson moved the following resolution:

"Whereas it is our duty to contend for truth and justice, if any gentleman brings a charge against the character of a man, whether present or absent, and cannot substantiate the fact by good proof, he is chargeable with immorality, and is unworthy of public confidence."

Laid on the table for further consideration

The motion by Mr. Smallwood yesterday, respecting the supplies from abroad, was called up for adoption, and laid over till the afternoon session.

The Convention then adjourned.

Session V

Wednesday August 4th 3 p.m.

Mr. Smallwood's resolution was again brought up, and a long discussion took place. The motion was supported by Messrs. Smallwood, Dunlop, Warren, Watson, Counter, Liles, and Blanknort; and opposed by Mr. J. Henson. On division it was carried, viz: *Yeas*, Messrs. Dunlop, Liles, Smallwood, Freeman, Cannon, Warren, Ramsay, Ferris, Watson, Counter, Elmsley, Stringer, and J.T. Henson— 13. *Nay*, Mr. J. Henson— 1.

The Convention then adjourned to Thursday.

Session VI

Thursday August 5th 9 a.m.

Mr. Henson's resolution was taken up, as already given... The following amendment was then offered by Mr. Smallwood, and adopted by the meeting:

"Whereas it is our duty to contend for truth and justice, and if any gentleman brings a charge against the character of any man, whether present or absent, whose public acts are not shrouded in mystery, thereby creating suspicion against his character, which he cannot substantiate by good proof, he shall be charged with immorality, and be held unworthy of public confidence."

## Session VII
## Thursday August 5th 3 p.m.

*Resolved*, That whereas the British American Institute in the Township of Dawn, Canada West, is not conducted to the satisfaction of the People of Colour in this Province, a Committee of five members of this Convention be appointed to audit the books and papers of said Institution...

*Resolved*, That all coloured people in Canada be recommended to become freeholders as soon as they have an opportunity of doing so, as a legitimate means of increasing their influence in the community.

*Resolved*, That this Convention recommend to all their brethren throughout the Province to tolerate nothing but truth in their intercourse with the world— to be quiet and peaceable subjects— and to avoid all cause of censure or reproach from those around them...

## Session VIII
## Friday August 6th 9 a.m.

*Resolved*, That the coloured people of Canada are not in the degraded state in which they have been presented by some of the pretended Agents who have gone out...

*Resolved*, That among the best means for improving the moral, religious, and social condition of our peole are Common and Industrial School education, and instruction in the truths of the Word of God...

Mr. J. Henson then rose and proceeded to satisfy the Convention in regard to his agency for the British American Institute. He handed his book to the Secretary, with an account of his intromissions since the 1st March last. This was read over to the Convention, and it showed clearly that Mr. Henson had faithfully discharged his duty to the Institution.

It was then

*Resolved*, That the Convention is satisfied with the conduct of Mr. Henson, so far as they have heard from him.

Convention then adjourned.

Session IX
Friday August 6$^{th}$ 3 p.m.

*Resolved*, That these Minutes be printed, and that each copy shall not exceed 4 1/2d, that 1000 copies be printed, or 1500 if necessary, and that the proceeds shall go to defray the expenses of the next Convention.

# BIBLIOGRAPHY


Bearden, Jim and Butler, Linda Jean. *Shadd: The Life and Times of Mary Shadd Cary*. Toronto: NC Press, 1977.

Bentman, Raymond. *Robert Burns*. Boston: Twayne Publishers, 1987.

Bliss, Isabel St. John. *Edward Young*. New York: Twayne Publishers, 1969.

Bunson, Matthew. *Encyclopaedia of the Roman Empire*. New York: Facts on File, 1994.

Burns, Robert. *The Poems and Songs of Robert Burns, Volume II*. James Kinsley, ed. Oxford: Clarendon Press, 1968.

Byron, Lord. *The Complete Poetical Works*. Jerome J. McGann, ed. Oxford: Clarendon Press, 1986.

Campbell, Thomas. *The Complete Poetical Works of Thomas Campbell*. J. Logie Robertson, ed. Oxford: Oxford University Press, 1907.

Chase, Harold W. et al, eds. *Dictionary of American History*. Revised Edition. New York: Charles Scribner's Sons, 1976.

Clarke, George Elliott. "Must All Blackness Be American?: Locating Canada in Borden's *Tightrope Time*, Or Nationalizing Gilroy's *The Black Atlantic*." *Canadian Ethnic Studies*. 28:3 1996 56-71.

Clogg, Richard. *A Concise History of Greece*. Cambridge: Cambridge University Press, 1992.

Cooper, Lane, ed. *A Concordance to the Poems of William Wordsworth*. London: Smith, Elder & Co., 1911.

Cowper, William. *The Poems of William Cowper, Volume II 1782-1785*. John D. Baird and Charles Repkamp, eds. Oxford: Oxford University Press, 1995.

Curran, John Philpot. *Speeches of the Right Honourable John Philpot Curran, Master of the Rolls in Ireland*. Third Edition. Dublin: J. Duffy, 1868.

Danckert, Stephen C., ed. *The Quotable Johnson: A Topical Compilation of His Wit and Moral Wisdom*. San Francisco: Ignatius Press, 1992.

Davies, Norman. *Heart of Europe: A Short History of Poland.* Oxford: Clarendon Press, 1984.

Davis, Charles T. and Gates, Jr., Henry Louis. *The Slave's Narrative.* New York: Oxford University Press, 1985.

____________________ "Introduction: The Language of Slavery." *The Slave's Narrative.* New York: Oxford University Press, 1985, xi-xxxiv.

Elwell, Walter A., general ed. *Baker Encyclopaedia of the Bible.* Grand Rapids, MI: Baker Books, 1988.

Firth, Edith, ed. *Early Toronto Newspapers: 1793-1867.* Toronto: Baxter Publishing/Toronto Public Library, 1961.

Flanders, Stephen A. and Flanders, Carl N., eds. *Dictionary of American Foreign Affairs.* New York: Maxwell Macmillan, 1993.

Fleischner, Jennifer. *Mastering Slavery: Memory, Family, and Identity in Women's Slave Narratives.* New York: New York University Press, 1996.

Hagelman Jr., Charles W., and Barnes, Robert J., eds. *A Concordance to Byron's Don Juan.* Ithaca, NY: Cornell University Press, 1967.

Hagen, Edith P., ed. *The Columbia Granger's Dictionary of Poetry Quotations.* New York: Columbia University Press, 1992.

Herold, J. Christopher, ed., trans. *The Mind of Napoleon: A Selection from His Written and Spoken Words.* New York: Columbia University Press, 1955.

Homer. *Iliad.* Trans. Richard Lattimore. Chicago: University of Chicago Press, 1952.

Howard-Hall, T.H., ed. *The Comedy of Errors: A Concordance to the Text of the First Folio.* Oxford: Clarendon Press, 1969.

____________________ *Cymbeline: A Concordance to the Text of the First Folio.* Oxford: Clarendon Press, 1972.

____________________*Julius Caesar: A Concordance to the Text of the First Folio.* Oxford: Clarendon Press, 1971.

Ingram, William and Swain, Kathleen. *A Concordance to John Milton's English Poetry*. Oxford: Clarendon Press, 1972.

Johnson, Thomas J., ed. *The Oxford Illustrated Companion to American History*. New York: Oxford University Press, 1966.

Lavater, Johann Caspar. *Essays on Physiognomy: Designed to Promote the Knowledge and Love of Mankind*. Twelfth Edition. London: W. Tegg, 1862.

Leick, Gwendolyn. *Who's Who in the Ancient Near East*. New York: Routledge, 1999.

Lewis, Walker, ed. *Speak For Yourself, Daniel: A Life of Webster in His Own Words*. Boston: Houghton Mifflin, 1969.

Longfellow, Henry Wadsworth. *The Complete Poetical Works of Henry Wadsworth Longfellow*. Boston: Houghton, Mifflin and Company, 1893.

March, Jennifer, ed. *Cassell Dictionary of Classical Mythology*. London: Cassell, 1998.

Metzger, Bruce M. and Murphy, Roland E., eds. *The New Oxford Annotated Bible*. New York: Oxford University Press, 1996.

Miller, Floyd J. *The Search for a Black Nationality: Black Emigration and Colonization 1787-1863*. Chicago: University of Illinois Press, 1975.

Miller, Randall M. and Smith, John David, eds. *Dictionary of Afro-American Slavery*. Westport, CT: Praeger, 1997.

Milton, John. *Paradise Lost*. Second Edition. Scott Elledge, ed. New York: W.W. Norton, 1993.

*The National Cyclopaedia of American Biography*. New York: James T. White, 1896.

Naugle, Helen Harrold. *A Concordance to the Poems of Samuel Johnson*. Ithaca, N.Y.: Cornell University Press, 1973.

Neve, John. *A Concordance to the Poetical Works of William Cowper*. New York: Greenwood Press, 1969.

*Niagara Falls, Canada*. Kiwanis Club of Stamford. 1968.

Nichols, Charles H. "The Slave Narrator and the Picaresque Mode: Archetypes for Modern Black Personae." *The Slave's Narrative.* Charles T. Davis and Henry Louis Gates, Jr., eds. New York: Oxford University Press, 1985, 283-297.

Olney, James. "'I Was Born': Slave Narratives, Their Status as Autobiography and as Literature." *The Slave's Narrative.* Charles T. Davis and Henry Louis Gates, Jr., eds. New York: Oxford University Press, 1985, 148-174.

O'Neill, Michael. *Percy Bysshe Shelley: A Literary Life.* London: Macmillan, 1989.

Page, Norman. *A Byron Chronology.* London: Macmillan, 1988.

Pease, William H. and Pease, Jane H. *Black Utopia: Negro Communal Experiments in America.* Madison: The State Historical Society of Wisconsin, 1963.

Reid, J.B., ed. *A Complete Word and Phrase Concordance to the Poems and Songs of Robert Burns.* New York: Russell & Russell, 1967.

*Report of the Convention of the Coloured Population Held at Drummondville, Aug., 1847.* Toronto: Printed at the Banner Office, 1847.

Ripley, C. Peter et al, eds. *The Black Abolitionist Papers: Volume II Canada, 1830-1865.* Chapel Hill: The University of North Carolina Press, 1986.

Robertson, Norman. *The History of the County of Bruce.* Toronto: J.M. Dent & Sons, 1960.

Saltzman, Jack; Smith, David Lionel; West, Cornel, eds. *Encyclopaedia of African-American Culture and History.*Toronto: Prentice Hall, 1996.

Shadd, Mary A. *A Plea for Emigration.* Richard Almonte, ed. Toronto: The Mercury Press, 1998.

Shelley, Percy Bysshe. *The Works of Percy Bysshe Shelley, Volume I.* Harry Baxton Forman, ed. London: Reeves and Turner, 1880.

Silverman, Jason H. *Unwelcome Guests: Canada West's Response to American Fugitive Slaves, 1800-1865.* New York: Associated Faculty Press, 1985.

*Speeches of Henry Lord Brougham, Volume I.* Philadelphia: Lea and Blanchard, 1841.

Stephen, Sir Leslie and Lee, Sir Sidney, eds. *Dictionary of National Biography*. Oxford: Oxford University Press, 1963.

Stouffer, Allan B. *The Light of Nature and the Law of God: Antislavery in Ontario 1833-1877*. Baton Rouge: Louisiana State University Press, 1992.

Strong, James, ed. *The New Strong's Exhaustive Concordance of the Bible.* Nashville: Thomas Nelson, 1996.

*Toronto City Directory*. 1846-1883.

Tytler, Graham. *Physiognomy in the European Novel: Faces and Fortunes.* Princeton, N.J.: Princeton University Press, 1982.

Walcott, Rinaldo. "Rhetorics of Blackness, Rhetorics of Belonging: The Politics of Representation in Black Canadian Expressive Culture." *Canadian Review of American Studies*. 29:2 1999 1-24.

Walker, David. *Appeal to the Colored Citizens of the World*. Herbert Aptheker, ed. New York: Humanities Press, 1965.

Wells, Stanley, ed. *Oxford Dictionary of Shakespeare*. New York: Oxford University Press, 1998.

Winks, Robin. *The Blacks in Canada: A History*. Second Edition. Montreal: McGill-Queen's University Press, 1997.

Williams, John. *William Wordsworth: A Literary Life*. New York: St. Martin's Press, 1996.

Wordsworth, William. *The Poetical Works of William Wordsworth*. E. DeSelincourt and Helen Darbishire, eds. Oxford: Clarendon Press, 1954.

Young, Edward. *Night Thoughts*. Stephen Cornford, ed. Cambridge: Cambridge University Press, 1989.

# AUTHOR'S ACKNOWLEDGEMENT

This book would have been impossible to complete without a trip to Ithaca in New York State, where the only extant copy of Smallwood's *Narrative* is held. I'd like to thank my friend Shelly Chagnon both for making the trip to Ithaca with me, and for making it possible in the first place. At the Carl A. Kroch Library at Cornell University, Lucy Burgess, Rare Book Assistant, and Lorna Knight, Curator of Manuscripts, were exceedingly kind and helpful.

— *R.A.*